New
Ceramics

New Ceramics

edited by
Eileen Lewenstein
and
Emmanuel Cooper

VNR VAN NOSTRAND REINHOLD COMPANY
New York · Cincinnati · Toronto · London · Melbourne

Acknowledgements

We are grateful to the contributors and to the many people
and organizations who have co-operated most helpfully in
the preparation of this book. Unsigned contributions have
been compiled from information given by individuals and
national organizations. Special thanks are due to Hugh
Wakefield and David Coachworth of the Victoria &
Albert Museum, London, and to Henry Rothschild, Jan
de Rooden, Jacques Blin, John Davis and Kurt Spurey.
The following organizations have provided pots, addresses,
photographs and advice:
The British Craft Centre, London
The Craftsmen Potters Association of Great Britain,
London
The Crafts Advisory Committee, London
Chambre Syndicale des Céramistes et Ateliers d'Art de
France, Paris
Indian Studio Potters Association, Bombay
Ceramic Artists Association of Israel, Tel-Aviv
Department of Information, Pretoria, South Africa.

Many of the illustrations have been specially commissioned, others sent by contributors, by individual potters
and by organizations. Photographic credits (where known)
are included in the captions. Special thanks are due to the
Victoria & Albert Museum for permission to reproduce
the black and white photographs by Geremy Butler
which were specially commissioned for the 1972 International Ceramics Exhibition held at the Museum.

All references are to height except where otherwise
indicated. Where two or more objects are
illustrated the height applies to the tallest.
Figure references in the text are to caption numbers.

Van Nostrand Reinhold Company Regional Offices:
New York Cincinnati Chicago Millbrae Dallas
Van Nostrand Reinhold Company International Offices:
London Toronto Melbourne
Copyright © 1974 pp. 1–22, 31–224 by Eileen Lewenstein and
Emmanuel Cooper
Copyright © 1974 pp. 23–30 by Tony Birks
Library of Congress Catalog Card Number 74-2590
ISBN 0-442-21647-5

Printed in Great Britain
Published in the United States of America in 1974 by
Van Nostrand Reinhold Company
A Division of Litton Educational Publishing, Inc.
450 West 33rd Street, New York, N.Y. 10001
16 15 14 13 12 11 10 9 8 7 6 5 4 3 2 1
Library of Congress Cataloging in Publication Data
Lewenstein, Eileen.
  New ceramics.
  Bibliography: p.
  1. Pottery. I. Cooper, Emmanuel, joint author.
II. Title.
NK3930.L48   738'.09'04   74-2590
ISBN 0-442-21647-5

Contents

Contributors

Eileen Lewenstein and **Emmanuel Cooper** are co-editors of, and regular contributors to, the magazine *Ceramic Review* which they started for the Craftsmen Potters Association in 1970. Both serve on the Council of the Craftsmen Potters Association, and both have work in the collection of the Victoria and Albert Museum.

Eileen Lewenstein is an established potter who, with Brigitta Appleby, formed Briglin Pottery in 1948. Since 1959 she has made ceramic objects as well as pots. Her work has been exhibited widely in several countries, and she was a participating member of the International Ceramic Symposiums held in Bechyne, Czechoslovakia in 1970 and Memphis, Tennessee, USA in 1973. She was a member of the Organizing Committee of the International Ceramics Exhibition held at the Victoria and Albert Museum in 1972.

Emmanuel Cooper has a workshop in London where he makes mainly domestic stoneware. He has had many exhibitions in Britain and has been represented in exhibitions abroad. He is the author of *A Handbook of Pottery* (Longmans 1970), *Taking up Pottery* (Arthur Barker 1971) and *A History of Pottery* (Longmans 1972).

Tony Birks trained as a painter and sculptor at the Slade, and as a potter at the Central School in London. After taking an Oxford degree, he taught pottery and sculpture at the Oxford School of Art and later at the Hampstead Pottery in London. His studio is at Sherborne in Dorset. Interested in all forms of design, both ancient and modern, his books include *The Art of the Modern Potter*, *Building the New Universities*, *The Potter's Companion* and *Meyer's Handbook of Ornament* (ed.).

Paul Köster runs the Gallery Ludker Köster at München Gladbach and has developed it from an antique gallery to the leading showcase for German ceramics. A good eye and a willingness to promote new talent has earned him an important place in the German ceramic world.

Patriciu Mateescu was born in Romania and studied at the Institute of Fine Arts at Bucharest. He shows work regularly at international exhibitions including those held at Vallauris, Faenza and London. He is secretary of the Union of Fine Arts of Romania.

Karin Wallin is a Finnish textile designer. She worked for a time as exhibition planner and architect at the Finnish Design Centre in Helsinki. At present she divides her time between designing and freelance journalism, and is also studying sociology at the University of Stockholm. She lives partly in Sweden and partly in Finland.

Nino Caruso is the director of the International Ceramics Centre in Rome. He is an individual ceramist and designer for the ceramic industry, whose work has been awarded many prizes in both national and international exhibitions. At present he is working on a series of decorative modular units for architectural use.

Ismail H. Oygar is Professor of Ceramics at the Academy of Fine Arts, Istanbul. He had been responsible for much of the present development of ceramics in Turkey, and is a member of the committee of the International Academy of Ceramics.

Gwen Sands studied ceramics at the Central Technical School in Toronto, Ontario, and now has her workshop in Toronto. She is editor both of *Tactile*, the magazine published by the Canadian Guild of Potters, and of *Craft Dimensions – Artisanales*. She is a member of and is active in the World Crafts Council.

Paul S. Donhauser is Professor of Art at the University of Wisconsin where he teaches ceramics, design and philosophy of art. His work is represented in many American collections and he has contributed articles to *Craft Horizons* and *Ceramic Review*.

Kimpei Nakamura studied sculpture at Kanazawa Art University and glazing techniques at the Japanese Government Industrial Research Institute. He teaches at Tama Art College. His work has been widely exhibited at home and overseas and he has contributed many articles to Japanese and American magazines. In 1970 he was guest editor of *Craft Horizons*.

Wanda Garnsey studied pottery at the National Art School, Sydney, is a member of the Potters' Society of Australia and is founding editor of the Society's magazine *Pottery in Australia*. She is co-author of the recently published book *Australian Pottery*. Her pots are in state collections in Melbourne and Sydney.

Introduction

New Ceramics is an illustrated survey of what is happening in studio pottery today. During the last decade many potters have become involved with new concepts. In some instances they have continued to make traditional wares and their creative involvement has been with formulating new clay bodies and glazes and investigating neglected firing techniques. Other potters however have moved away from making utilitarian articles and are now solely concerned with producing art objects. It is the purpose of this book to illustrate these new developments.

Studio pottery is a general term and can include a whole range of ceramic objects from useful domestic wares to sculpture. It can best be identified by the methods and attitudes with which the work has been made rather than the objects themselves. Studio potters or, as they are sometimes called, ceramists can be individuals working alone in their own workshops, in which case their output tends to be very small, or they can employ a team, of usually six to ten people, who work under their direction. Many of the articles they make could be mass-produced industrially but studio potters enjoy being closely involved with their materials and are on the whole reluctant to relinquish control of the making processes to machines.

This material involvement, so strong in pottery, goes some way to explain the attitude of the artist who works with clay. A studio potter, whether he produces cups and saucers, decorative objects or sculpture, will maintain that he is equally concerned aesthetically with any object through his material. In one way his attitude is similar to that of an earlier time, for instance Ancient Greece, when craftsmen were classified according to the materials they used rather than the objects they produced. For example a mason worked with stone and was concerned with its quarrying and eventual forming into buildings or statues; similarly with artists using wood, metal and clay. Perhaps this diversity of aptitudes has remained with the clay worker longer than with other craftsmen because of the complexities of the basic technical knowledge required for finding, fashioning and firing clay.

Studio pottery comes out of a society that is essentially a result of the industrial revolution. Mass-production techniques enabled basic consumer demands for such things as crockery and sanitary ware to be easily satisfied, but the uniformity of machine made goods soon led to a desire both from the manufacturer and the purchaser for objects that possessed some mark of individuality. The pottery industry therefore employed painters and modellers to apply 'art' to their wares and, in some instances, set up special art departments or studios. This somewhat muddled reaction to the machine caused a new value to be placed upon an article made by hand.

It was not long before the artist potter was born. Many of these early studio potters were absorbed in discovering the technical secrets of wares recently imported from the Far East, whose glazes were quite different from any previously known in Europe. Other potters protested against the advent of the machine, on the grounds that its soulless efficiency was deadening and that it caused social disruption.

The pattern of development in studio pottery has differed in each country and has depended on many factors, but it is always closely connected with reactions to industrialization. The value of comparing work from many countries is evident both from the contrasts and similarities which can be observed. Each of the main sections in this book has an introduction by some-one with an intimate knowledge of the work being made in those countries so as to provide a useful background to the illustrations; some countries however are represented by photographs only. The picture presented by the individual contributors is in each case a personal one, for as Karin Wallin of Sweden points out another author could well have provided a different view of Scandinavian ceramics. The rest of this introduction will give a background to the subject as a whole without going in detail into the whole history of pottery as that has been done elsewhere.

The industrial revolution saw changes in methods of production whereby one man and a machine could produce in a day as many goods as several men working by hand for many days. Different machines were devised for different craft techniques and the craftsman replaced by the machine operator. Initially the pottery industry retained its established methods of throwing and turning and was content to speed up production by division of labour and cut-throat piece-work rates. Before long it was realized that greater quantities of ware could be produced by less skilled and therefore less expensive labour, if slip casting or jolleying into plaster of Paris moulds was used as the principal method of manufacture. Demands from the newly emerging middle class for low priced but refined and delicate ware could easily be met by small factories and this caused the country potteries, formerly producing a vigorous but comparatively coarse slipware, gradually to decline.

It is interesting to note that at this time there was a distinction in status between the pottery workers who actually made the objects and those who painted the decorations on them. Contemporary prints always show the decorators at work in high collared frock-coats; they were the 'artists', already a cut above the craftsmen.

It was against this background of great industrial change and technical innovation that the Great Exhibitions of the nineteenth century were set. Here different nations displayed their achievements and vied with each other to produce ever more splendid examples of the technical virtuosity of their machines, which could not only produce articles in quantity, but could also help to provide the elaborate ornamental detail that became the hallmark of Victorian decorative art. The first such exhibition was held in London in 1851 at the instigation of the Prince Consort. In Britain the national collection of decorative arts, now known as the Victoria and Albert Museum, was founded on profits from that exhibition.

Other exhibitions followed in European and American capital cities to encourage competitive trade. It was soon realized that some assistance was needed in training artists and designers if local manufacturers were to compete satisfactorily with those in other countries. Art schools were established throughout the industrialized world in order to train the designers and artists necessary for a viable manufacturing economy. These schools carefully distinguished between fine and applied arts, sometimes to the extent of creating separate institutions for each.

However it was probably as true a hundred years ago as it is today that students in art schools regarded themselves as creative artists, whatever their discipline. It was only natural therefore that students studying ceramic design and decoration saw themselves as artists primarily concerned with producing art objects. While they might only have been trained in designing a suitable shape to be made and in applying the decoration, they saw themselves as creatively involved.

As a result a handful of individual artist craftsmen emerged from European and American art schools, who could support themselves partly by their designs for factories and partly through their own production. Sometimes an exploration of decorative techniques would prove a starting point for new work. At other times they would turn for inspiration to the wares of another period or country. In a sense these artist craftsmen were protesting against the uniformity and sterility of machine made goods, but they couched it in terms of applying 'art' from the outside. Seldom were they really involved with the techniques of making the objects from beginning to end.

Within this context mention should be made of Doulton's of Lambeth, England, one of a number of factories who set up special departments to produce what became known as Art Pottery. Henry Doulton was keenly interested in this project and from 1862 onwards did much to encourage students from the nearby Lambeth School of Art to come and work in his factory; he laid particular stress on the necessity of accurate observation of nature for the basis of pleasing design. Hannah Barlow and George Tinworth were associated with this company for a long time.

At that time a Frenchman, Jean-Charles Cazin (1841–1901), known both for his painting and stoneware pottery was teaching at Lambeth. He there met and worked with Robert Wallace Martin (1843–1923) the eldest of the four Martin brothers, probably the first artist potters in England. Robert was originally a stone carver and went to Lambeth School of Art to study modelling; it was here that he developed a lasting interest in pottery. Two of his younger brothers, Walter and Edwin, also studied at Lambeth and then worked at Doulton's before joining him to produce their very individual saltglazed wares. Many of these pieces were based on grotesque animal forms, but they also produced simpler, attractively decorated pots. With a fourth brother Charles they maintained production at Southall, Middlesex until 1914.

Other factors affected the development of studio pottery. During the second part of the nineteenth century foreign trade with the Far East had increased dramatically. New trading agreements made with China and Japan meant that their artefacts were brought to Europe in quantity for the first time. These newly imported high fired stonewares were particularly influential in France where there was already a general enthusiasm for the art of the Far East, especially that of Japan. The rich textured glazes were of great interest to potters whose knowledge of coloured glazes was very limited. Stoneware glazing in Europe had until then been largely confined to the addition of salt during the firing; a few metal oxides had been used to colour the wares but this only allowed a very limited range of effects. The desire to reproduce these glazes became an obsession for some potters.

At that time there was little knowledge of the chemistry and physics of ceramics available. For the most part the early French studio potters were forced to find things out empirically, either by working in the traditional country potteries or gaining what knowledge they could from the large porcelain factories. One of the first of these potters, Theodore Deck (1823–91), learnt from both sources and saw that artists and industry had to co-operate. He succeeded in producing reduced copper red glazes on porcelain at Sèvres and his work received great acclaim at the Paris exhibitions of Decorative Arts. In 1887 he was appointed director of the Sèvres factory. Other French potters of that period who should be mentioned are Ernest Chaplet (1835–1909) who was apprenticed at Sèvres and later endeavoured to produce Chinese type glazes, and Emile Decoeur (1876–1953) who carried out valuable experiments in glazing high fired stonewares. It was with Chaplet that Paul Gauguin did his ceramic work from 1886 to 1888. There has always been more collaboration between potters and painters in France than in other countries. Potters would often invite painters to decorate their pots, but this collaboration between equals was entirely different from the way in which the artist potter decorated the pot thrown for him by his employee.

In England the Arts and Crafts movement viewed the industrial revolution as the greatest self-inflicted disaster ever perpetrated by mankind. This movement with its ideals of truth to materials and respect for human labour could only see the machine as degrading to humanity. As a result they regarded the imagined way of life of the mediaeval craftsman as an ideal and many pioneers set off for the countryside to put their theories of craftsmanship into practice. William Morris was the most influential thinker associated with the movement, and many societies were formed where his ideas were discussed and methods sought whereby the work of artist craftsmen could be brought before the public to encourage sales or commissions for new work. The Arts and Crafts Exhibition Society was formed especially to promote their work and held its first exhibition in 1881. This society is one of the many that still exist today; in response to changing circumstances it is now known as the Society for Designer-Craftsmen.

Yet, pottery was not one of the crafts greatly affected by this movement. William de Morgan, a personal friend of William Morris, attempted to apply his ideas of design and decoration. But he was influenced by Persian and Islamic pottery and spent most of his time trying to discover ways of reproducing these glazes and colour effects. He established a workshop in London where he produced pottery but mainly concentrated on decorating tiles. He was however successful in discovering methods for producing reduced lustres on tin glazed wares.

By the beginning of this century it was possible to discern in Europe differing attitudes towards artist potters and their work, which, although slightly modified, still persists to this day. In China and Japan pottery has always been considered an art form of equal value to painting and sculpture, while in Europe this was not the case. But possibly because the main influence on continental artist potters came from the Orient some of the accepted values of the East came with it. As a result artist potters found that art galleries were prepared to handle their work. These potters were primarily concerned with making one-off pieces and their attitude to the work was similar to that of an artist in any other field.

In England the situation was slightly different. The Arts and Crafts movement had extolled the virtues of the humble anonymous craftsmen producing simple, useful articles for everyday use. Such objects they thought could have no place in an art gallery, since they were everyday things and were produced in quantity, modest as those quantities were. As with any idealistic movement there was some difference between theory and practice; the simple, useful articles could never be produced at a price low enough for the ordinary working man. Fundamentally, the refusal to come to terms with the machine meant that an opportunity for influencing industrial design was lost, while their emphasis on the hand-made, craft aspect of their wares acted to the detriment of the market value of the work produced. Art could be sold in galleries, but craftwork could only be sold in exhibitions or shops, and consequently at much lower prices. Indeed it was not until the early 1920s that one English potter, William Staite Murray (1881–1962), was able to cross the barrier between craft and fine art in having his vigorously thrown pieces exhibited at the Lefèvre Galleries in London. Each of his pots was given a title and the prices were comparable with those asked for painting and sculpture. His aim was for the acceptance of pottery as a medium of expression on a par with other fine arts.

Well into the beginning of this century, the Schools of Art continued to be one of the factors influencing the development of studio pottery. It was still difficult for artist potters to acquire technical knowledge. At this point their main interest lay in glazes and particularly in reproducing the stoneware ones of the Far East, although they were often fascinated by wares from other countries. The knowledge that had been built up within the pottery industry, although available through the few art schools with pottery departments, was not immediately relevant to their problems, for the main aim of the factories was producing pure white clay bodies, which would be covered by a thin layer of well fitting transparent glaze; decoration was printed or hand painted, and the colours used were finely ground and clear of hue. Often gold and silver were applied with yet another firing.

Yet studio potters needed strong stoneware clays still full of the natural impurities that the industry so carefully extracted, to which glazes could be applied thickly and unevenly and which would give interesting colour and texture effects. It was also essential to them that they should get to know the behaviour of their materials under varying firing conditions in the kiln. There was a continual need for experiment, especially as there was a reluctance to share knowledge once it had been acquired.

Books on the subject were few and far between and in any case mainly written from an industrial point of view. Emile Bourry's *A Treatise on Ceramic Industries*, first published in 1901, contained much useful information and was later supplemented by Alfred B. Searle's *Clayworker's Handbook* (1906). Richard Lunn wrote a book entitled *Pottery*, published in 1903, as a handbook for teachers and students. There was certainly some published information but scarcely enough to enable an ill equipped potter to undertake considerable further research himself.

In Europe the influence of Michael Powolny (1871–1954), Professor of Ceramics at the Academy of Applied Art in Vienna, was widespread; students came to Austria from all over Europe and subsequently returned to their own countries carrying his teaching with them: the chemistry of ceramics was included in the curriculum. Helena Johnova (1884–1962) of Czechoslovakia was a pupil of Powolny. In 1919 she was appointed Professor of Ceramics at Prague School of Applied Arts and it was largely due to her influence that studio pottery has developed so strongly in Czechoslovakia. Vaclav Markup (b.1904), Julie Horova (b.1906) and the present Professor of Ceramics in Prague, Otto Eckert (b.1910), were all her pupils.

In England art schools continued to provide training for designers and decorators rather than makers of pottery. At the Royal College of Art, a comprehensive syllabus based on industrial techniques was firmly established by Richard Lunn, who had been appointed instructor in 1903. Students were not usually taught to throw, a skill they were unlikely to need, and a technical assistant, usually a thrower from the potteries, was employed to make shapes to students' designs. Courses were available at other London colleges such as the Central School of Arts and Crafts, founded in 1894, and at the Camberwell School of Arts and Crafts founded in 1898. Charles Vyse studied at Camberwell and later, helped by his wife Nell, produced interesting examples of Chinese stoneware glazes. He also designed a gas kiln that was a great advance for studio potters because of the degree of control possible over the rate of firing and atmosphere in the kiln.

Charles Binns, 1857–1934, an English potter trained at the Royal Worcester Porcelain Company, emigrated to the USA and settled in New Jersey. Appointed director of a trade school for ceramics in 1900, he soon established for himself a reputation as educator, ceramic technologist and individual potter so that he was made the first director of the New York School for Clay at Alfred University, later known as the New York State College of Ceramics. This has continued to be the leading American school for ceramic education and research.

It was still the general practice for students to learn to design shapes and decorate them. If on leaving college they set up their own studios to produce pots they would employ a thrower, as the studio or artist potter was still concerned with the appearance of the piece rather than its making. Like the former frock-coated decorators in the potteries, the studio potters could be considered artists, and their throwers craftsmen.

However, despite the lack of instruction in the technique of throwing students did acquire this knowledge. At the Royal College of Art in London, a group from Stoke-on-Trent succeeded in teaching themselves, and one of them, Dora Billington, was then appointed instructor after the death of Richard Lunn. There were of course other art school students who taught themselves to throw, most often by watching traditional throwers in the few remaining country workshops. Denise Wren (b.1891) was a design student at Kingston-upon-Thames School of Art in Surrey. She became intrigued with pottery and set about learning the technique of throwing from a local flowerpot maker. She was soon, in 1919, to establish her pottery in Oxshott, Surrey, where she lives and works to this day. She designed a simple yet efficient coke fired kiln, which made it possible for many potters to build and fire their own kilns at a reasonable cost. Once a fundamental interest in throwing had been established, studio potters turned more and more to traditional country potteries for inspiration and help.

It might be expected that a movement which at this point was largely based on the art schools would reflect new developments in other arts, but there is little evidence of this. It must be remembered that there was still a firm division between fine and applied arts and at this stage influences tended to come from other branches of the decorative arts. Art Nouveau with its flowing, linear style was quickly absorbed into the Art Pottery departments of the factories and mention could be made of, among others, Christopher Dresser in England, Alfred William Finch in Finland and of the Rookwood Pottery in the USA. It seems to have had little influence on studio potters although traces can be discerned in the work of the Martin brothers.

Art schools throughout the world were producing potential studio potters whose interest was gradually coming to include the making of pottery as well as its designing. The increased interest in throwing was making these potters receptive to the influence of the robust and vigorous wares of the mediaeval craftsmen which they had formerly tended to ignore. On the whole their output was small and they concentrated on pieces that were one of a kind. In continental Europe they saw themselves primarily as artists not craftsmen making pieces that were decorative rather than useful, while in England and the USA the distinction was less clear.

15

The end of the World War I saw a number of major and exciting developments in art and design, many of which were related to attempts to integrate them into society. In the USSR the immediate post-revolutionary period saw some short-lived but interesting attempts to produce a completely socialist visual environment. There was much theoretical discussion, and most of the work produced was of a very mechanistic nature, but a notable exception was the work of Tatlin; for a time he headed the Ceramic Faculty in Moscow and formulated a 'Culture of Materials' based on a study of organic life.

In Germany the Bauhaus (1919–33), under the direction of Walter Gropius produced a theory of design that considered the function an object was required to serve. The properties of materials were explored and students were encouraged to challenge traditional usage by finding new ways of handling or processing. This proved a stimulating factor and led to an exciting period in which there were many innovations in the field of design. It was in complete contrast with established methods of art education in which students were expected to accept and absorb without question any instruction they were given. It had a more immediate effect on crafts in continental Europe than elsewhere, and it was not until the flight of the former Bauhaus staff from Nazi Germany that its effect became far reaching, particularly in the USA, where many of them settled.

In Britain studio potters were to be influenced greatly by Bernard Leach after his return from Japan in 1920. Bernard Leach was born in China of English parents, educated in England and studied at the Slade School of Art in London where he learnt etching. Taking his etching press with him, he then travelled to Japan. While there he became interested in pottery which he learnt from the Sixth Kenzan, a traditional Japanese potter, and it was pottery that became his main concern in life. He decided to return and work in England, but with him came Shoji Hamada from Japan who helped him set up his workshop in St. Ives, Cornwall. It was there that Bernard Leach set about a fusion of traditional Japanese and English country pottery. He slowly introduced Japanese concepts of art and beauty, which are completely integrated with other aspects of life. He went to the roots of traditional English country pottery, and for the first few years the Leach Pottery was mainly concerned with producing a well designed range of domestic slipware closely based on traditional mediaeval shapes. There were occasional firings of stoneware.

But within this early period Bernard Leach was establishing the precepts that were to have a lasting effect on studio pottery: in making objects of the highest quality there could be no separation of the activities of artist or craftsman. All the different processes involved, from the initial consideration of functional and aesthetic aspects of design to preparing the clay, making the pot, decorating, glazing and eventual firing, were of equal importance – the artist and craftsman were one. At the Leach Pottery each potter was encouraged to make individual or one of a kind pieces as well as being involved with the production of standard wares. Gradually stoneware replaced slipware for all domestic products. In his work Leach successfully combines the intellectual qualities of Japanese appreciation of form and decoration with the practical approach of the traditional English potter – a fusion of East and West.

There are few studio potters today who have not been influenced by him at one time or another. Although he passed on his ideas to the many students who came to work with him at St. Ives, among them Michael Cardew and Katharine Pleydell-Bouverie, it was with the publication of *A Potter's Book* in 1940 that his influence became most widespread. Here for the first time was a book that dealt with all aspects of studio pottery: for many he has become a prophet and *A Potter's Book* has become a bible. He made the attractive proposition that it was possible for a potter in the twentieth century to set up a workshop and there produce, with his artist/craftsman's skill and the help of a few assistants, a range of domestic wares and individual pieces that the public would want to buy. It was a proposal that attracted many followers. His influence has been greatest in England, the USA, Canada, Australia and New Zealand – all English-speaking countries where a considerable market has been established for handmade domestic wares.

Studio potters in other European countries continued to be more closely connected with the pottery industry. Many of these potters, greatly influenced by the Bauhaus, found that their designs for mass-produced wares were readily accepted. Some firms such as Arabia in Finland and Gustavsberg in Sweden established studios within their factories where studio potters could work on individual pieces with all the technical resources of a large industrial concern at their command. In these circumstances the potter would conceive the desired end result and technicians would provide the clays, glazes and firing conditions necessary for its achievement. In other words, all the technical aspects of production were firmly under control. For Leach there were always some factors in production that were not quite under control: although the artist/craftsman is responsible for everything, yet, however well he knows his materials and his kiln there is always the possibility that some chance element could lead to a more beautiful and more interesting result. But the skill of the factory technician can remove that element of chance.

In many ways the studio within the factory is ideal. Here the potter has freedom to pursue his own creative ideas secure in the knowledge that he will be rewarded for his efforts. Many individual potters whose work is of great interest have emerged from such studios, for instance Stig Lindberg of Gustavsberg, Sweden, and Rut Bryk, of Arabia, Finland. But today the very success of this system has caused some of the younger potters in Scandinavia to view it with mistrust. For them such employment would mean acceptance of the established values of the consumer based society in which they live, and these values they find unacceptable.

The period since the end of World War II has seen a rapid expansion of studio pottery as a whole and also a widening of the terms of reference within which studio potters work. In the thirties there were relatively few studio potters working in most industrialized countries while today it has become an acceptable professional occupation, and an extremely popular amateur activity as well. How has this expansion come about?

At first it was very gradual. A potter setting up a workshop would take on a student as an assistant; after some two years the student would then leave and set up his own workshop, in his turn engaging an assistant, while the original potter would take on another student, and so on. Gradually there were more opportunities for students leaving college to practise their craft. Although some students opted for full-time potting, the majority chose to combine potting with teaching, or some other reasonably well paid part-time occupation. During the fifties art schools began to offer specialist courses for studio potters. Instruction was provided in a wide variety of making and firing processes and included the chemistry of ceramics.

The full-time potter, however, is usually forced to base his production on a range of easily saleable domestic wares; this can still allow time for making a number of individual pieces, but these tend to be restricted to the vocabulary of clays and glazes already available within the workshop. The part-time potter/ teacher/designer can more easily afford to experiment and is more likely to devote his time to pursuing ideas of form and colour through the exploration of clay as a medium of expression. Sometimes, as for instance in Germany, these experiments are closely related to the concept of the pot as a container. For other potters elsewhere, most notably in Japan and the USA, this concept has vanished and been replaced by the notion that an object, which might incidentally be a container, can only truly be said to be itself, or as some might say 'art'. All these different areas of interest are represented in some degree in all countries, but their proportions vary considerably from country to country.

Other factors must also be considered. In the early fifties Picasso went to live near Vallauris, a small pottery town in the south of France, and for about a year he threw his irrepressible creative energy into pottery. He was fascinated by the manipulative quality of the newly thrown pots which a local potter made for him and which he swiftly transformed into birds, people, or animals with a superb economy of means. He also decorated hundreds of dishes by gouging and scratching the surface, trailing and painting lively yet delicate patterns in slip or metal oxides, and by using brightly coloured glazes with the confident abandon of an assured artist. For a brief period he brought pottery before the public in a manner that some potters found shocking and others delightful. Picasso's direct influence on studio pottery was slight, but it was something of a stimulus to potters in France, as it led many painters to an interest in pottery and probably many potters to an interest in painting. Joan Miró was drawn to ceramics and worked on many different projects with Jose Llorens Artigas at his pottery in Spain.

Picasso's was not the only 'art' influence on studio pottery after 1945. The end of World War II saw a change in the concept of representational and abstract painting. In the late forties a group of American painters broke away from the idea of conscious art by splashing, dripping and pouring paint on

18

canvas in an attempt to capture some subconscious feeling in form and coherence. In this frozen action they tried to show some of the dilemma of modern life. From this style developed the so called 'pop' or popular art which, by incorporating everyday objects, gave them the status of art. It sought to magnify aspects of the contemporary environment and bring back an awareness of art to daily life. Both movements influenced potters, initially in the USA, but soon in Japan and all over the world. Such ideas were readily acceptable to potters because they showed that traditional concepts were not inviolate and materials were only as good as the use made of them. Clay, traditionally used to make pots or representational sculpture, was now used by these potters to make almost any sort of object. Its versatility and adaptability were exploited as ends in themselves. Pots made by traditional methods were broken or cut up and reassembled in any way other than to produce a useful object. Soft clay walls were pushed and pulled and the effects obtained were heightened by rich colours of majolica or lustre. In the USA the work of Peter Voulkos has probably had most influence in establishing a new set of values and attitudes to ceramics. His work originated in basic pottery forms and then moved completely away from the concept of the container to pure sculptural considerations. Paul Soldner, a potter whose name is inevitably linked with raku, has also done much to explore the visual and tactile qualities of clay as a medium of expression.

Nevertheless these influences from the world of painting did not mean that conventional pots were no longer made. In Japan the older and established studio potters such as Shoji Hamada, Kanjiro Kawai and Kenkichi Tomimoto continued to work within the strongly established Japanese tradition and their work was as highly regarded as ever. It was mainly due to Bernard Leach that in the period from 1920 to the beginning of the fifties throwing as a technique and stoneware as a medium were the dominant influence on studio pottery. This influence was so strong that other making processes and firing temperatures had tended to be ignored. By the late fifties, in exactly the same way that an earlier generation had reacted against their situation in order to learn how to throw, some potters were now intent on rediscovering industrial techniques and materials which were to become for them the starting point for a whole new series of explorations. Jacqueline Poncelet (31) and Glenys Barton (9) in England are recent examples of studio potters who have explored such techniques creatively with the use of slip cast bone china, a clay body usually associated with the English pottery industry.

By the sixties technical knowledge was easily obtainable. A generation of outstanding pottery teachers had managed to improve art school facilities, and had then been prepared to publish the results of their own investigations and research into methods of making, glazing and firing clay. Especial mention must be made of Daniel Rhodes's work at Alfred University, New York. His book *Clay and Glazes for the Potter* was published in 1957 and soon became a second potters' bible. It was followed by *Stoneware and Porcelain* in 1959 and *Kilns: Design, Construction, and Operation* in 1968. The Spanish potter Artigas published a book of glaze recipes in 1961 and Pravoslav Rada of Czechoslovakia published *A Book of Ceramics*. Informative books were now being published and translated into many languages and a number of magazines began to appear devoted solely to studio pottery. No potter could now plead ignorance through lack of available information.

Potters are now quickly aware of developments in other countries. The many well illustrated books and magazines concerned with studio pottery are one of the reasons for this, but there are also the international exhibitions and symposiums. The Annual International Ceramics Exhibition in Faenza, Italy is now a firmly established event. Vallauris in the south of France is sponsoring biennial exhibitions and the International Academy of Ceramics helps arrange large exhibitions which are held every few years in different countries. The list to date is impressive: France (1954), Belgium (1959), Czechoslovakia (1962), Switzerland (1965), Turkey (1967), Britain (1972) and Canada (1973). These exhibitions act as a focal point for current work and also reflect the interactions between the work of potters in different countries.

The International Ceramics Symposiums are working sessions in which a group of potters from different countries and usually with different languages will work within the same environment for a limited period, usually four weeks. This ideal opportunity for potters to gather and pass on information through their methods of work is easier and simpler through practical involvement than theoretical discussion.

Studio potters throughout the world work against a wide and varying background. At no point in their history have they been so well equipped to practise their craft, as a vast body of information relating to all aspects of ceramics is available and the results of further research are published promptly. Archaeological excavations provide new and sometimes unexpected findings in the techniques and artistic achievements of earlier cultures, and potters are made instantly aware of current developments in other countries. Like all other creative workers, potters have never been confronted with so many conflicting influences and stimuli. What then is the present situation?

Some potters, overwhelmed perhaps by such a wealth of opportunity, have gone to the extreme lengths of discarding all these hardly won advantages. These potters are rediscovering pottery making at its most primitive level. Others have decided to abandon all attempts to give permanence to their wares, which they leave to the mercy of the elements.

As Paul Donhauser points out in his introduction to work in the USA, studio pottery today falls loosely into three main categories, but as will be seen from the photographs in this book these are in no way related or limited to any one country. Firstly there are potters working in a traditional way, producing well designed and well made pots usually for domestic use. Secondly there are potters still working in a traditional way, but concentrating on making individual pieces, carefully and sensitively decorated; the functional aspect is subordinated to a decorative one. In the third category come the object makers and sculptors. For them clay is a means of expression and their interests range from abstract considerations of form to direct social comment.

New Ceramics shows work that is currently being made by studio potters all over the world. While the main development of the last decade has been the new area of concern that has arisen around the concept of the ceramic object, a final assessment of studio pottery needs to consider its relationship both to the pots of history and also the society in which it is made. Potters today have inherited a rich vocabulary of forms, colours and textures – a heritage which present technical knowledge is able to exploit to the full. But whether inspiration comes from the primitive soft wares of Nigeria, the lead glazed wares of mediaeval England, the sophisticated porcelains of the Far East or the 'coca cola' bottles and beer cans of contemporary life, these sources are the creative starting points of new explorations. Through their work studio potters can both comment on and contribute to the world around them.

Eileen Lewenstein
Emmanuel Cooper

London 1973

Britain

There has been a good deal of change in ceramics in the last decade, as a new generation has moved up alongside the mature potters of the sixties. Britain has not, however, become a focus of activity in ceramics, as might have been the case, and new directions are therefore centrifugal rather than self-centred. It seems that no country provides a united philosophy and a hard core of good ceramics in the way in which Japan, for example, or Korea did in days gone by. One has to look to a fairly primitive society or a peasant economy today to find the communal aesthetic in pottery-making which keeps standards vibrantly high. The more developed the country, the more diverse will be the outlook of potters, the more wide-ranging will be the work, and often the more confused will be the critique.

This applies to Britain and to America, and the principal direction noticeable in British ceramics in recent years has been a sidelong glance, especially by young potters, at what is being produced across the Atlantic. Certainly this does not mean that the best work is American-influenced, but rather that *some* work is American-influenced, while the rest is not influenced by other ceramics at all, and certainly not by whatever might be happening in other European countries.

What is new is that some potters commit themselves, vulnerably perhaps, to a newish concept – the art-object in clay. This concept, with its obtrusive and clamorous product, has drawn some attention away from the entrenched views of the orientalists and it readmits the figurative use of ceramics after a long period of neglect. The time has surely come for an assessment of the ceramic art object in terms of design, of its value as a means of expression compared to other forms and, rather important, of the potency of the views of those who choose to use and develop it. If this is, as it must be, the heart of any discussion of British ceramics today, then it must first be put in its context.

Britain is teeming with potters; professional, amateur, self-employed, part-time, and – a category of some standing and with enormous influence – the teacher-potters. These are people, of whom I have been one, who do not have to make their living by making pots, but have a great deal of time and some incentive to do their own creative work, cocooned from commercialism and very often favoured with exhibition space. As both facilities and gallery space have expanded, the work of these potters has become more and more exposed, and not surprisingly it is from this group that some of the art-object ceramics have come. The people concerned cannot be regarded as potters in the traditional, workshop, sense and in their creative work they undertake commissions or 'exhibition batches' as artists not as artisans. Whether this influence is good or bad, it is only to be expected that their work, which often benefits by the lighting and display facilities of the gallery, will be well to the fore in mixed exhibitions such as *International Ceramics 72* and *The Craftsman's Art* (1973), both held in London.

The extent to which a mixed exhibition shows the experimental tip of ceramics or, instead, a broad spectrum of work with different aims depends on the selectors' terms of reference, and to some extent this is affected by the expectations of the audience. Michael Sellers, who runs the Selwood Gallery at Frome, Somerset, has said 'The national percentage of people interested in the arts and crafts is no higher than five per cent. If we are to save the crafts from appealing to the initiated few, we must make inroads into the other ninety-five per cent . . .' Though five per cent means two or three million people in Britain, new ceramics which require a large, receptive audience still have to battle against attitudes which are not only slow to change but are often quite stubbornly confused.

Ask the average man in Britain what is meant by hand-made pottery and unfortunately he will still come up with the definition of the lowest common denominator pot; that which is more coarsely made than it would be if made in a factory, less useful, less efficient, more expensive and not necessarily beautiful at all. The ceramic which makes a social comment, which has a message or thumbs its nose at alternative ceramics, is left out of account (and therefore fails to get its message across) though the same general consumer would not require of every pot a function. For him it is enough for it to be part of a furnishing scheme, particularly if the pot is hand made, just as Toby jugs are not required to be jugs, or even satirical portraits, merely ornaments. There is, of course, a vast sub-structure of potters who make that for which there is a demand, and thus is perpetuated the idea that a lumpish handle put on badly can be excused, or even praised.

In this climate five hundred or more studio potteries operate successfully in Britain, and perhaps a hundred potters experiment seriously for a minority audience. The craftsman-patron relationship, which worked in ceramics as in other fields up to the industrial revolution, persisted in ceramics in a tenuous way until very recently, with certain potters producing the expected and the unexpected for collectors whose criteria were in the main aesthetic, and whose standards were high. Unlike the most important twentieth-century painters, a handful of potters of the first rank could be relied on to produce an elegant object, always of encompassable size, with distinct qualities which one could enumerate on one's fingers, and with a material link with tradition, giving time-lessness.

Now, while artist potters (including the art-object makers) become more like painters in their relationship with their patrons, official Government patronage has been set in motion in Britain to encourage the craftsman. In the light of this there is a need for a new assessment of craftsmanship. The amount of money involved in this state patronage is small – if it were put to use solely for the upkeep of craftsmen it would support, at the most, two hundred – but it is enough to make the definition of craft in the seventies important, so that there can be some guidelines for the distribution of the annual grant. Clearly, at one extreme it could encourage the learning of high skills in antiquated techniques unrelated to modern living; at the other it could be accused of supporting the dilettante in making useless objects of no function and no beauty. In practice, one of the objects of this patronage is to help the unestablished with the capital costs of establishing workshops and of course ceramics is only one of several fields which are eligible.

If state aid is not to be indiscriminate, some selection has to be made, and it is most likely that this will be based on artistic 'promise' rather than proof of 'craftsmanship'. Unfortunately definitions of the craftsman and craftsmanship lead into a circular argument as the role of the potter changes or the potter's assessment of himself is modified. The definition 'well made by hand' will certainly no longer do, for one must ask 'well made in what context?' 'Made from start to finish by a single hand' separates the artist and craftsman from the industrial designer, and creates an albeit artificial barrier for the ceramist who wants his work to get a wide showing. It is easy to get involved in a semantic argument to no purpose, but the matter cannot be ignored, for 'good craftsmanship' – whatever this may mean – is still regarded as a desirable quality by the various bodies in Britain which serve the interests of the potter. It is an emotional term which arouses strong feelings in people who are incapable of defining its meaning.

Clearly certain practical qualities are an advantage to certain pots, especially functional ones, but the presence or absence of these qualities is often irrelevant in the appraisal of the individual work; it all depends on the pot. Signs of craftsmanship such as 'good joints', implying stability, are essential for the furniture maker, but it is impossible to formulate them for the potter. The special skills in putting on handles, ensuring pure bodies, perfect pouring, non-scratchy bases, etc., are those which industrial ceramists must learn in order to survive. The craftsman potter may learn them too, and must do so if he is to compete with industry, but they are only practical skills and not to be equated with aesthetic sensitivity and delicacy of rendering.

It is not so much in pursuit of the chimera of craftsmanship alone, but rather with the intention of providing practical skills that a down-to-earth course, teaching the hardware, software and carpentry of pottery has had such success at Harrow School of Art, achieving international renown in less than a decade. Its aim is to prepare the student to become a self-sufficient workshop potter, with all the skills necessary to develop his talent, though he may be no great shakes as an artist. The problem of placing such emphasis on practical skills is that inevitably the emphasis is removed from aesthetics, and indeed it is the intention at Harrow that well articulated, functional ware should reinforce the functional aesthetic and that additional emphasis on design is unnecessary.

Most of the work at this leading school is thrown. While no one would doubt the usefulness of throwing in the teaching of pottery, or the majesty of a superb contemporary wheel-made pot, the potter's wheel is a background to new directions in ceramics, rather than the active and obvious tool; voluptuous thrown pots are exceptional in Britain today. A pot taken at random from a market in southern Europe or northern Africa and placed amongst an average collection of thrown ware in Britain will make them all appear stiff and contrived, self-conscious and mannered. Peasant potters, non-existent in Britain, who still make domestic ware for a living (I am not referring to the potters who serve the tourist industry with marginally functional or totally 'decorative' absurdities), have a fluency and an ability to create *beautiful* ware without striving, which is beyond the reach of the intelligent artist potter in this country. The grace and undoubted aesthetic value of the contemporary 'amphora' shows how aimless are most British wheel-made pots which hover uncertainly between usefulness and beauty as a result of the loss of tradition and traditional roles for thrown ware. Not all new thrown work in Britain is so disappointing, and the work of Michael Casson (22) for example, is excellent by any standards.

The touchstone of the humble amphora, rigorously applied to help in the evaluation of thrown ware in general, is helpful in reducing pretentious and essentially imitative pots to their true status. I cite this touchstone only as an example of graceful, relaxed and confident throwing, not as a functional prototype. Indeed, I think there is something absurd about cider-flagon making in the modern British environment, and only justified by an exceptional work. To make matters worse, the British retail trade does not help either the consumer or producer by commissioning such pots for immediate adaption as table lamps.

A backcloth or perhaps a chorus of thrown pottery of varying quality therefore spreads across the stage of ceramics in Britain, against which the outstanding and the new is exposed to view, and we can now return to the original assessment of the 'art-object'.

Clay has an amazing capacity for responding to the potter's intentions, and in the last few years it is the expressive possibilities of making ceramics which *represent* things which have come to the fore. Traditionally pottery is abstract in that it is not 'like' anything; it justifies itself as a hollow form, with or without function; it is not figurative and it certainly need not be representational, even in its decoration. The ceramic art-object, on the other hand, is both. There has been a rediscovery of the fact that clay can imitate – with breathtaking realism – lace, human skin, the patent leather of a shoe (with gilt buckle), or the cracked leather of an old satchel. The technical skill involved in this representational form is considerable, but when the object is made it is no longer self-justifying like the pot, and into the satchel may go ceramic sandwiches or hand-grenades. Immediately the ceramic takes on the potential of a satirist's or a propagandist's weapon, or becomes the vehicle for a child-like fantasy. As in sculpture and painting, much interest is taken by potters in expendables: plastics, reinforced cardboard packaging and vacuum forming. The ceramics produced represent boxes, milk bottles, typewriters and the like, and sometimes infinite care is spent over re-creating in permanent ceramic form that overrated pathos of the neglected, broken toy. What might be called the headless-doll syndrome in pottery appears to me as a rather unseemly self-indulgence by potters who prefer to refer to their limited pasts than to their limited futures. The fantasy does not need to be child-like, and clearly a material which can create a strong illusion can have a powerful effect. The illusion by itself is fairly meaningless, like throwing lines without a pot, but it makes the art-object a medium of communication, like a drawing or a photograph.

The reason the result is so often unsatisfactory is that the message does not get across to a big enough audience, or perhaps that it is not worth hearing. As a medium for communication, ceramics must lose out against other media in practically every way except for tiresome longevity. They are seen by a minute audience compared to film, television, the written word or the cartoon, and only rarely are they monumental enough in scale to allow them to be mounted in public places. Yet to put a strident ceramic art-object with a message to tell away in a cupboard will diminish it, for the more 'relevant' the pot the more its meaning will fade with the passing of time. The dynamic life-span of individual examples of this essentially long-lasting art form has become briefer, in common with other art forms; last year's talking point gathers dust in the way that only ceramics can gather dust. Social and political comments are short-lived in their impact and they give to ceramics the kind of adrenalin that kills.

In the two-dimensional arts, especially the graphic arts of communication, the artist must apply rigorous selection until his message is clear and uncluttered. He is forced to take design decisions, even if political or emotional expression is his chief intention. In ceramics the need for deliberate design decisions is less obvious. Two hands clasped in friendship and cast from a plaster mould make their own design; the slip-cast balaclava shapes itself. Furthermore a great many of the symbols used in art objects are themselves the products of intensive design exercises, so that the potter reduces himself to the role of stage manager or impresario. The classic example of this is the Union Jack, irresistible as a piece of graphic design, fascinating when distorted, waving, or frozen in mid-air, pounced upon as a symbol by object makers, or simply used in a self-deprecating way as a ready-made design for silk-screening on cubes and cylinders.

A natural progression for the ceramic art-object could be towards mechanical means of reproduction so that, like the 'twopence coloured, penny plain' popular art of two hundred years ago, it could be mass-produced and absorbed by a large audience. It is, however, very often just exactly the mass-marketing techniques that the art-object is satirizing so that when one specially made (and dented) Coke tin is reproduced a thousand times, and each dented tin reduced to a reasonable price, the world has gone completely upside down, and once again we are in souvenir land.

The communicator is not interested in the archetype, and the art-object maker is probably concerned with essentials and origins, and so the possible future route of multiple production is more probably a blind alley.

What, therefore are the qualities to be sought in the ceramic art-object, on the assumption that it is at least allusive, if not truly representational? Should its 'impact' be equated with beauty if the former removes the possibility of grace, pattern, harmony or proportion? A great many art-objects are not beautiful or harmonious by traditional standards. Instead they are arresting or disgusting, and because of their capacity to arouse a response in the viewer, they are rarely boring. Most of them use the form itself as a means of expression, rather than allowing the surface to be a vehicle for a painted or drawn design, though there is no reason why this needs to be the case; it so happens that currently artist-potters in Britain are more closely allied to the sculptor than to the painter. The outstanding art objects made today are conceived sculpturally. Their design is closely controlled. The marriage between form and surface or glaze is an appropriate one, and they are sensually satisfying.

These criteria for appraising the figurative pot are thus the same as would distinguish a superior, traditional (or abstract) ceramic from its dull, unsensual, inelegant fellows. One is not dodging the issue by assessing in traditional terms a medium which is now used to communicate ideas. It is simply that ceramic art-objects which do not have sculptural and tactile qualities are less interesting than those which do.

The most fluent and uncompromising of the art-object makers in Britain is Anthony Hepburn (i, 27), whose progress from pottery skittles, through cast telephones, to unfired polythene bags of moist clay, has alarmed or maddened many people. Making a show is part of his way of life and the enduring quality of a ceramic is irrelevant to him. As striking objects, his pots are outright winners in any competitive assembly. A ceramic can be dashing and obtrusive without having any value, but most of Anthony Hepburn's work is simple and sculptural, which, combined with the materials of which it is made, gives it the permanent quality which interests me, if not the artist himself. He uses whatever techniques will produce the exact result he requires, without any respect for ceramic traditions, and by calling attention to a variety of industrial processes his work expresses the technique he employs as perfectly as the throwing lines mark the hand of the thrower.

Graham Burr (iii), a more mature purveyor of the heavy ware of pottery, creates major ceramic forms with a combination of what might seem to be incompatible techniques. His simple sculpture, often repeating mathematical forms, is decorated using the technique of the photo-retoucher, and then fired to stoneware temperatures. The burly shapes are eerily nebulous in their decoration, though he shares with Hepburn the decisiveness which make his pots stand out both in exhibitions and in private collections. In a decade starved of pottery decorators, the work of Graham Burr is outstanding for the precise complementary balance between form and decoration.

Another potter working on a similar scale, and with an equally precise attention to detail is Gordon Baldwin (3). In his hands the art-object is earthenware, shiny, and usually black. It hints at representation in a rather sinister way, since the dark shiny objects often resemble the lethal tools of modern warfare. Such a romantic view is typical spectator reaction to work which, though carefully planned, is not entirely integrated in ceramic terms.

The truly representational object comes from artists like Alan Barrett-Danes (34), who aims at realism to confound the eye, and who manages to create by the surfaces he achieves on clay, that most tactile of materials, a positive anti-tactile reaction. Amongst many younger artists making art-objects in clay, Andrew Lord (36) is another interesting potter who produces sculpture which relates ceramic precedent with humour.

28

There are several major British potters, particularly those using slab techniques, whose current work is allusive, though not entirely naturalistic. Outstanding is Bryan Newman (25), who has developed as an artist both inventive and sensitive. Producing reduced stoneware ceramic sculpture, mainly from slabs, as well as deftly handled and 'modified' thrown forms, he has moved from fantasies in tableware – which do not endear him to traditional potters – to more complex, non-ceramic subjects such as boats and townscapes. His most recent pots, made of very large slabs meant to stand on the floor like shields, are truly sculptural in scale and feeling. Although they are so varied, Bryan Newman's ceramics are unmistakeable.

Ian Godfrey (2) is another potter with a very distinctive ceramic handwriting, but in his case there is a strong oriental influence: figurative fantasy pots, boxes with landscapes on their lids, farm animals, each with an allotted place in a stoneware farmyard. These appealingly simplified animal forms dominate his current work. In concert with them he makes magnificent stoneware bowls with perforated designs and cut rims.

Alan Caiger-Smith (38), standing quite alone, and for that reason sometimes left out of account, directs his energy to the ornamentation of pottery forms in the majolica tradition. If other potters had his ability to handle a brush and fill a space with lively pattern decoration, then painting on pottery would not have come so close to extinction in Britain. Not for him the contemplative oriental brushmark, but rather the near-symmetry and abstract pattern of Moorish and Persian designs. His recent experiments in 'real' or Persian lustre are entirely appropriate, and his work lies comfortably within the traditional frame of useful ware without having lost its ability to give joy and exhilaration.

A rising interest in porcelain forms, whether cast, hand-made or derived from the wheel, is well exemplified by the work of Jacqueline Poncelet (31), Mary Rogers (iv, 29) and Eileen Lewenstein (16). Mary Rogers has for some time been associated with delicately folded pinched forms, and is now increasingly using natural and biological themes in her small elegant sculptures. This artist first became a master of her medium; she is now showing her creative powers. Eileen Lewenstein's porcelain is based on thrown forms, sometimes modified into sculptural pieces of great beauty. She also makes more rugged sculptural pots, and the balance of her work invites comparison with Ruth Duckworth (177a & b), who, sadly for Britain, left England to live in the USA in the 1960s.

Of American origin, but extremely widely travelled and now working in Britain, is Janet Leach, whose forceful stoneware pots are amongst the most important being made in Britain today. High standards are to be expected of anyone associated with the distinguished Leach family (20, 24, 30), and the breadth of her experience in all forms of pottery seems to be combined in every single pot she makes, without loss of originality or vigour. Illustration 24 shows a pot which draws ceramic tradition through its pores, and exhales sculpture.

Continuously pursuing a course to an ever more perfect form, the work of Lucie Rie (4) stands out today above that of other potters as it has done for the last twenty years. She does not point to a new direction in ceramics (though her ceramic forms do not repeat themselves) but rather sets a standard in quality and harmony. The one constant factor is the tension or 'spring' in her thrown shapes, which keeps them always fresh.

Linked with Lucie Rie's work in the pursuit of purity of form are the very different ceramics of Hans Coper (ii). These abstract vessels, always in a state of development, I admire more than any other contemporary pots. They seem to demonstrate an awareness of the world's pains and poignancies without the need for allusion or representation. They have a perfect combination of originality and grace; they are desirable and yet aloof, and they relate to the present and the future more than to the past. If, forewarned of some imminent disaster, one had the opportunity to grab a single ceramic from Britain for posterity, hopefully it would be one of the pots of Hans Coper. A problem for a potter is how to justify a lifetime making ceramics in a changing Britain which does not need them as vessels, and which should not be offered them as trifles. The pottery of Hans Coper provides such a justification.

Tony Birks

London 1973

30

2

3

32

2 IAN GODFREY
Two-part container 1973, stoneware with matt white glaze, 17 in. Photograph by Alphabet & Image

3 GORDON BALDWIN
Landscape 1972, black glazed earthenware, width 14 in.

i ANTHONY HEPBURN (Britain)
Tall forms 1972, stoneware, 24 in.
Photograph by Ted Sebley

4

5

4 LUCIE RIE
Bowl 1972, porcelain, brown and bronze glaze,
sgraffito decoration, 4 in. Photograph by Crafts
Advisory Committee

5 PAUL ASTBURY
'*The Lizard and the Machine*' 1972, stoneware, 8 in.

6 ROBERT FOURNIER
Object 1972, stoneware with green glaze in centre,
width 12 in. Photograph by Ted Sebley

7 SHEILA FOURNIER
Bowl 1971, stoneware with torquoise glaze, width
12 in. Photograph by Ted Sebley

6

7

ii HANS COPER (Britain)
Three pots 1972, stoneware. Photograph by
Alphabet & Image

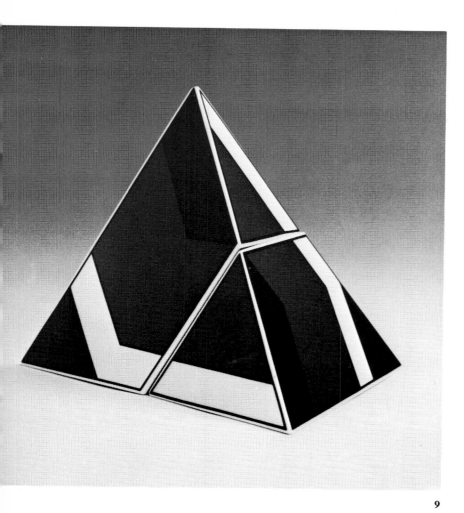

8 WALTER KEELER
Vases 1972, stoneware, 7 in. Photograph by
Ted Sebley

9 GLENYS BARTON
Bisected tetrahedron 1972, slip cast bone china
with on-glaze transfer decoration, 4 in.

10 MO JUPP
Pots 1973, stoneware, press moulded, pink
glaze, 10 in. Photograph by Ted Sebley

9

10

*

11

12

13

11 COXWOLD POTTERY (PETER DICK)
Casserole 1973, red earthenware body, slip decoration, wood fired kiln, 7 in. Photograph by Ted Sebley

12 ANDREW RICHARDSON
Pots 1973, saltglaze stoneware with white slip, 5 in. Photograph by Ted Sebley

13 DEREK DAVIS
Object 1973, stoneware, width 8 in. Photograph by Walter Gardiner

14

15

14 VICTOR MARGRIE
   Bowl 1969, porcelain, carved decoration, 4 in. Photograph by
   Crafts Advisory Committee

15 EMMANUEL COOPER
   Landscape object 1973, stoneware, incised decoration with
   white slip, brown pigment and blue green glaze, width 5 in.
   Photograph by Ted Sebley

16 EILEEN LEWENSTEIN
   Vases 1973, porcelain with incised decoration, 5 in.
   Photograph by Ted Sebley

16

17 EWEN HENDERSON
Pot 1973, stoneware, slip and oxide decoration, 12 in.
Photograph by Ted Sebley

18 KEITH WALLIS
'*Hill*' 1973, reduced stoneware decorated in green and
brown, 13¾ in. Photograph by Geremy Butler

19 RICHARD BATTERHAM
Lidded jar 1972, stoneware with green ash glaze, 8 in.
Photograph by Richard Hubbard

20 DAVID LEACH
Pot 1972, porcelain with red pigment rubbed into crackle,
white matt glaze, 4 in. Photograph by Ted Sebley

21 JOANNA CONSTANTINIDIS
Pot 1973, stoneware with black glaze inside, matt white
outside, 5 in. Photograph by Ted Sebley

18

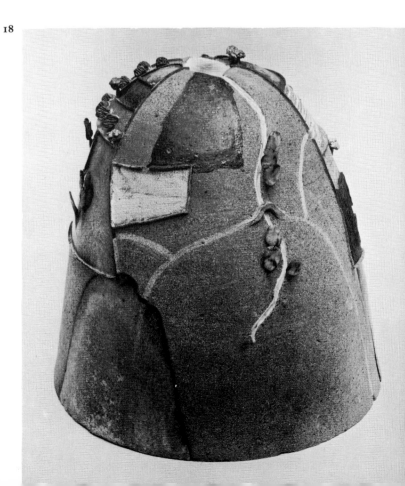

19

20

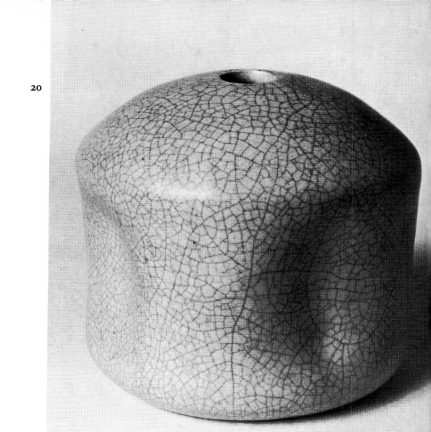

21

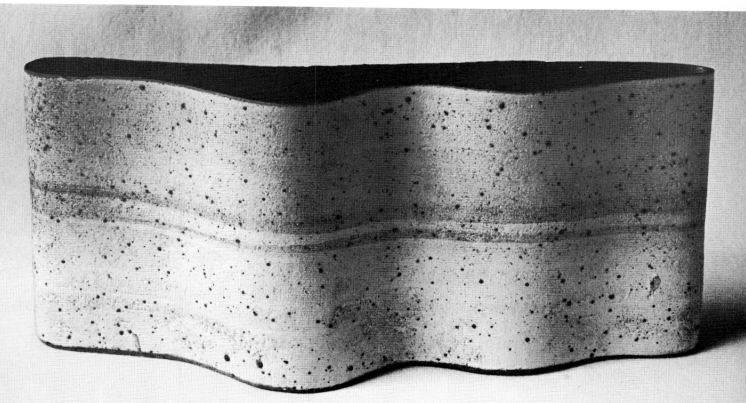

23

22

24

42

25

26

22 MICHAEL CASSON
Jug 1972, reduced stoneware, tenmoku glaze over red slip with combed decoration, 11 in. Photograph by Crafts Advisory Committee

23 MARIA GALLEN (Ireland)
Pot 1972, earthenware body with leaf decoration and blue, green and yellow glaze, 6 in. Photograph by Geremy Butler

24 JANET LEACH
Pot 1973, reduced wood fired stoneware, 8 in. Photograph by Ted Sebley

25 BRYAN NEWMAN
Three gondolas 1973, stoneware, slab built with matt glazes, 7–9 in. Photograph by Alphabet & Image

26 OLDRICH ASENBRYL
'*Alarm Clock*' 1973, stoneware, 10 in. Photograph by Ted Sebley

27 ANTHONY HEPBURN
Two Cups 1973, porcelain and stoneware, transparent glaze and silver lustre, 4 in.

27

28 TONY BIRKS
Tetrahedrons 1973, stoneware, various
glazes, 7 in. Photograph by Alphabet
& Image

29 MARY ROGERS
'Hollow Hills' 1972, carved porcelain,
3 in.

28

29

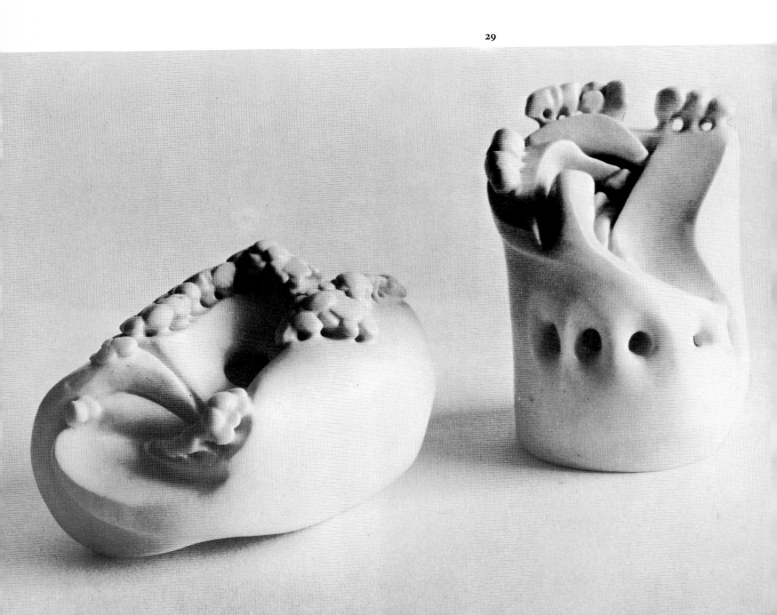

iii **GRAHAM BURR** (Britain)
Three half-cone variations 1972,
reduced stoneware, 24 in. Photograph by
Geremy Butler

30

30 BERNARD LEACH
Vase 1972, stoneware with fluted decoration, tenmoku glaze, 12 in.

31 JACQUELINE PONCELET
Bowl 1973, bone china, carved decoration, unglazed, 3 in.

31

46

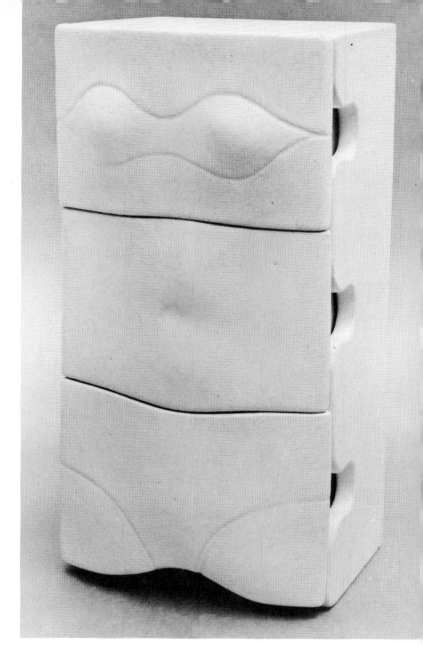

32 ADRIAN CHILDS
    '*Three Drawer Chest*' 1972, earthenware body with matt
    white glaze, 14 in. Photograph by Geremy Butler

33 GEOFFREY SWINDELL
    Pot 1972, porcelain, incised decoration, sand blasted
    glaze, 3 in.

33

32

47

iv MARY ROGERS (Britain)
Bowl 1973, porcelain, 3 in.

34 ALAN BARRET-DANES
'*Fungi with Courting Toads*'
1972, earthenware body
with sprayed slip and lustre,
8 in. Photograph by Geremy
Butler

35 PETER SIMPSON
'*Fungi Forms*' 1972, porcelain
with black and grey glaze,
width 7 in.

36

36 ANDREW LORD
Teapot 1973, earthenware
with oxides sponged on, 8 in.

37 JONATHON ATKINSON
Toy 1972, earthenware, 4 in.

38 ALAN CAIGER-SMITH
Bowl 1973, earthenware,
tawny orange lustre on
greyed tin glaze, width 11 in.

37

38

Scandinavia

In March 1972 a group of nine Danish ceramists arranged an exhibition entitled 'To be a potter today' at 'Den Permanente' in Copenhagen. The exhibition highlighted the problems common to craftsmen in all Scandinavian countries in recent years, for the Danish ceramists raised the question 'Are we, the producers of individual objects, really needed in a society characterized by overproduction, in a world already too centred around the object and its possession?' This question had engaged craftsmen during the sixties and had led to a partial paralysis of creative activity. It was hotly debated in the art and design schools and led to many changes. The same period had also seen the cult of the 'buy-use-and-throw-away' attitude which, in retrospect, seems demoralizing in its lack of respect for materials and its total lack of concern for objects and for nature.

The most confusing and difficult times are now over. They were in one sense a challenge for ceramists and have resulted in a greater feeling of responsibility towards, and a greater feeling of integration with society. The confusion forced ceramists to question their own position and define their attitudes, and this has led them to adopt clearer positions.

In a sense the question raised above provides its own answer. Artist-craftsmen are needed to keep the traditions and skills of craftsmanship alive in the industrial age of computers and plastics in which we live. Craftsmen can provide the individual care for materials and objects in a technical age; they can interpret dreams through materials such as clay in a period when efficiency, mass-production and commercial viability tend to be the only factors taken into account. Craftsmanship allows free and vital experiment in an age of endless repetition and mindless conformity, and for individuality in an age of anonymity. It provides an alternative to the 'buy-and-throw-away' syndrome, a more human way of evaluation than that of overconsumption.

New directions in Scandinavian ceramics of the seventies have arisen because of the need for such an alternative, sometimes in a conscious way, but perhaps more often instinctively. The crises of the last decade have led some of the object makers to see that the product as product is less important. One of the new tendencies has been that the cult of the object as such has lessened and a greater importance is attached to the object's message, to what it says and symbolizes. The Scandinavian ceramist of today is often not just a creator of perfectly shaped bowls, he is often also a sculptor, a surrealist, a realist, a naïvist, a pop artist, a story-teller, a person who shakes you up, a person who unmasks. This naturally does not mean that all aesthetic considerations are disregarded, but simply that ceramists have widened their terms of reference and have reached outside the boundaries of the concrete object as such. It has meant liberation at a time when other arts and crafts have developed towards freedom. This emergence of ceramists into the fields of fine arts as sculptors and as experimental artists is notable throughout Scandinavia, perhaps mostly so in Sweden, but also in the other countries; for instance in the work of Anna-Maria Osipow (54) in Finland with her sculptures influenced both by pop art and surrealism, Dagny (52) and Finn Hald (vi), Yngvild Fagerheim, Terje Westfoss in Norway with their many monumental works, and Sten Lykke Madsen (41) in Denmark with his stoneware bodies. There are no boundaries left. Free sculptural ceramics predominate over bowls, pots and useful wares.

The confusion and paralysis of the sixties was strongly connected with fear and a feeling of threat, threat against our whole humanity, our nature, our surroundings. The unpleasant side effects of production in a consumer-based society in the form of litter and pollution, in the destruction of the environment, was and still is too obvious to be ignored. For instance, one can see this threat expressed in the stoneware seagulls by Henrik Allert (44) of Sweden. A feeling of solidarity with the developing countries has also emerged and with it an interest in folk-arts and crafts. Catharina Kajander (53) in Finland for example started using her local red clay for her big, often surrealistic sculptures. She also made an inventory of folk-potters in Finland still using traditional materials. In a similar vein are the folk-based, humorous, and naïve ceramics by Ulrica Hydman-Vallien (49) in Sweden. Alev Siesbye (42), a Danish ceramist from Turkey, loves the simple round pregnant forms and the colours of her native south, which are like the earth, brown, yellow, rust and beige.

Other potters work on the wheel, throwing bowls and pots in strong traditional shapes, but they too are concerned that the craftsmens' position in society should be recognized. Some collective workshops and groups have been established such as the Plus workshops in Fredrikstad in Norway, from which prototypes for industry are also provided.

Political awareness among artists became more evident during the sixties. Many craftsmen now consider society as a whole to be more important than individual expression. One such artist is Britt-Ingrid Persson in Sweden who comments in clay with savage clarity. In one piece (45) a blind man busily blows air into a balloon depicting the world which bears a notice saying 'For Sale'. Despite the fact that social problems still exist, and force many ceramists to put protests and fears into clay, it still seems that part of the answer for craftsmen and artists can be found in the problem itself, in the wasteful use of resources in an industrial society. One answer is that of Catharina Kajander and others who work on an unobtrusive scale.

The 1972 exhibition in Copenhagen was arranged partly as a sandy beach with natural stones and big, soft, eternally floating ceramic formations, but also included the less pleasant, sharp-edged jetsam of our time, such as plastic products and packings. Ursula Munch-Petersen showed work in which she seemed to have peeled off the outer form and functions of the ceramic material and so let it be reborn on a sandy beach, to be seen completely naked among the other perishable materials of our times – in contrast to the fired clay objects, whose durability makes them seem almost eternal.

One of the most famous ceramist-sculptors in Sweden, Hertha Hillfon (47), combines successfully in her work the use of light and shadow, space and volume and air. In a piece called *The Child*, by carefully depicting only the wrap or cover she manages to convey clearly the warmth of a human baby seeking human contact.

Britt-Ingrid Persson's use of ceramics is simply as a medium for three-dimensional works; she wants her material as such to be anonymous. Her pieces are mostly matt-glazed, fairly plain stoneware, since beautiful glazes would take away a part of what she wants to express, and would render the pieces less disturbing. Her intention is to limit the reactions and the questions to the message she is trying to convey, a message which is often a biting criticism of society, but usually conveyed with an irony and humour, warm and typical of her character.

Something of an opposite yet very close relationship to the material can be found in a ceramist like Märit Lindberg-Freund (46), Sweden. For almost all her sensitive ceramics she uses white or very pale glazes. Sometimes she achieves effects like sheets of white cloth flitting in the wind with soft and delicate movements. Her work invariably has an attractive, tactile quality and a certain sensuality.

Erik Pløen (50), Norway, makes sturdy down-to-earth stoneware, tempting to touch, and strong in form and appearance; it repays close study. The forms are simple and decorated with rich colours, applied in several layers which shine through each other to give many shades of great richness.

Zoltan Popovits (57), in Finland, made lustrous ceramics plates when he worked as a guest-artist at the Arabia factories some time ago. He seemed to let them grow organically, piece by piece, by adding leaves or petals of clay to the forms, square and round at the same time. The pots were then covered with glowing shades of shining blacks and whites, pink, silver and mother of pearl. As well as plates he also made pop sculptures.

Birger Kaipiainen (58), of Arabia, Finland, specializes in ornamental pieces though he has also made designs for mass-production. In his work he uses thousands of earthenware beads, covered in many coloured glazes, and sometimes combines bits of mirror with larger areas which are then finished with a mother of pearl effect.

There are as many different ways of working in ceramics as there are ceramists, and as many ideas and ways to express them. Since the ceramists of Scandinavia work very much as individuals, it is not easy to group them into categories or to classify them according to the borders of their countries. No longer can one say that something is very typically Finnish or that that is the way the Norwegian potters express themselves and their 'national temperament' nor is it possible to describe in simple terms how most Danish ceramists work today. To do such a thing would be to destroy and take away individuality and to ignore the personal in favour of the national.

I have tried to give a general picture of the common features of ceramics in the Scandinavian countries and have had of necessity to leave out some of the artists working here. I have left it for the reader to judge if ceramics from the Scandinavian countries are different from new ceramics in other parts of the world. In this book the reader can use the pictures and accounts as a means of comparison. One might, however, add one reservation. The image of Scandinavian ceramics today could naturally have been different, if the choice of individuals had been different. The possibilities are many. Scandinavian ceramics are more diverse than these few pictures can suggest.

Karin Wallin

Stockholm 1973

Denmark

39

39 CHRISTIAN POULSEN (Denmark)
Bowl and plate, stoneware. Photograph by
Inga Aistrup

40 LISBETH MUNCH-PETERSEN (Denmark)
Bowls 1972, made in white china by Bing and
Grondahl. Photograph by Rigmor Mydtskov

41 STEN LYKKE MADSEN (Denmark)
Object 1972. Photograph by Leif Nielsen

40

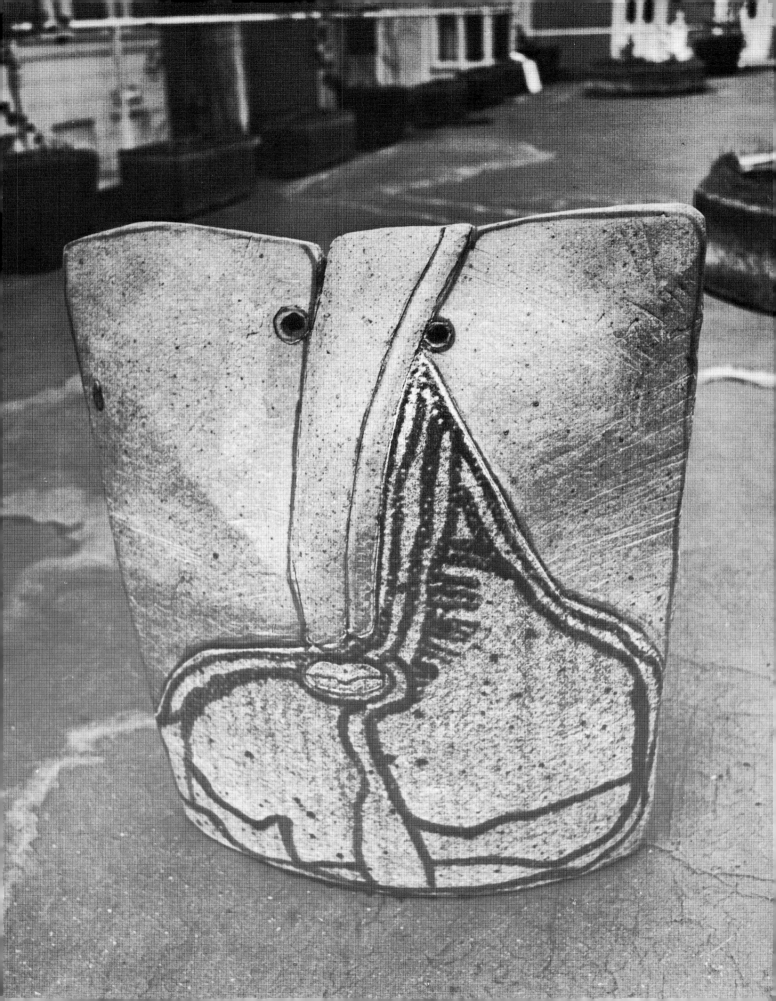

42

43

42 ALEV SIESBYE (Denmark)
Round bowls 1972

43 FINN LYNGGAARD (Denmark)
Plate 1972, stoneware with grey-white glaze and transfer design, width 18 in.

Sweden

44 HENRIK ALLERT (Sweden)
'*Seagull*' 1972, stoneware

45 BRITT-INGRID PERSSON (Sweden)
'*Balloon for Sale*', stoneware with
white surface, 24 in. Photograph by
Beata Bergstrom

44

45

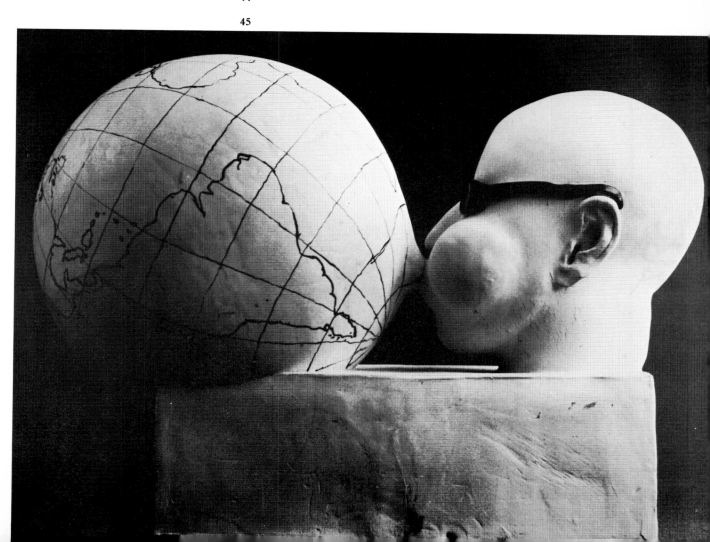

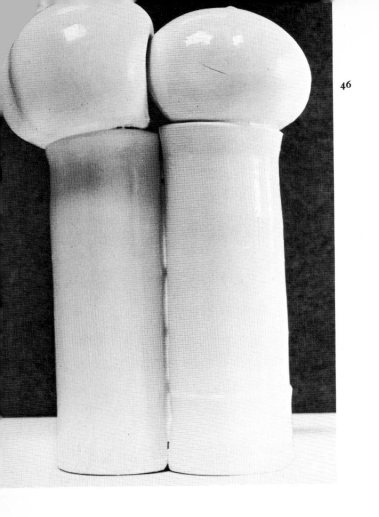

46 MARIT LINDBERG-FREUND (Sweden)
'*The Twins*' 1972, stoneware body with white glaze

47 HERTHA HILLFON (Sweden)
'*The Child*' 1972, unglazed stoneware, length 18 in.

47

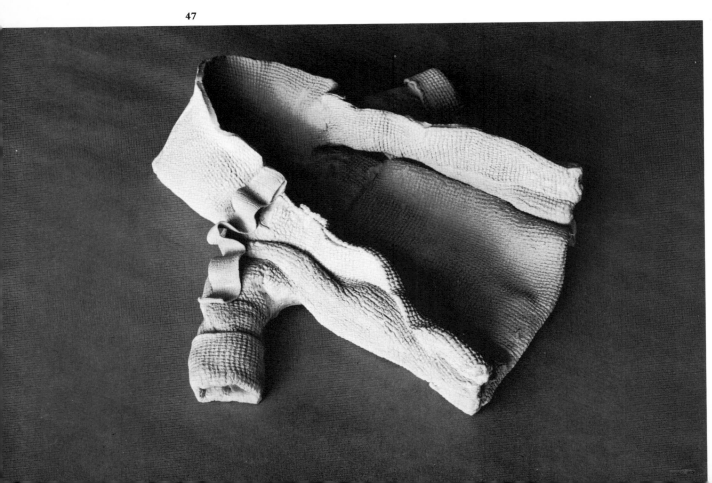

v LEIF HEIBERG MYRDAM (Norway)
  Forms 1972, reduced stoneware and porcelain

48 NILS GUNNAR ZANDER (Sweden)
   '*Mask*' 1972

49 ULRICA HYDMAN-VALLIEN (Sweden)
   '*Angel Protection*' 1972, earthenware body with white
   glaze, decoration in black and red brown, 14 in.
   Photograph by Sten Robert

vi FINN HALD (Norway)
'*The Peace Monument*' 1972, stoneware

50

Norway

51

50 ERIK PLØEN (Norway)
Vase 1972, stoneware with green grey and
brown glaze, 10 in.

51 ANNE-MARIE BACKER MOHR (Norway)
Pot 1972

52 DAGNY HALD (Norway)
'*The Lady with the Dog in the Wood*' 1972,
glazed stoneware. Photograph by Jan Larsen

52

Finland

53

54

55

53 CATHARINA KAJANDER (Finland)
'*The Lion's Mane*' 1968, red earthenware body, about
2 ft. Photograph by Ilmari Koistiainen

54 ANNA-MARIA OSIPOW (Finland)
'*With leather trousers on*', stoneware, medium fired,
39 in. Photograph by Esa Pyysalo

55 MARJATTA LAHTELA (Finland)
Sculpture 1972, stoneware with thin glaze, length 12 in.

56 PAUL ENVALDS (Finland)
Sculpture 1972, stoneware, made at Arabia factory

57 ZOLTAN POPOVITS (Finland)
Shallow plates stoneware in black, white, mother of
pearl, silver and pink glazes, made at Arabia factory,
about 3 in.

58 BIRGER KAIPIAINEN (Finland)
'*Sunrain*' 1972, 3 × 8 yds

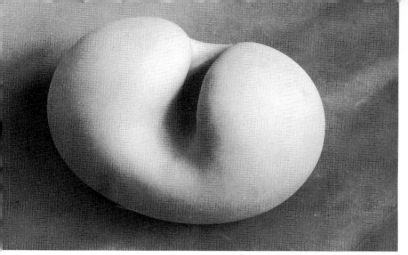

56

57

58

France
Holland
Belgium

France is the traditional mother of studio pottery, for it was here in the second half of the nineteenth century that artist potters started to work. Stimulated firstly by the imported Japanese wares, they made stoneware with rich, deep glazes. Later they moved away from the oriental traditions, especially with regard to forms and decoration, and instead found more inspiration in the work of the easel painters, often collaborating with them.

The work of the French artist potters was rated almost as highly as that of the fine artists and a firm tradition of exhibiting in galleries rather than shops was established which continued well into the thirties. In the period between the wars the scope of artist potters broadened and included more figurative work. Figurative decoration was incised in the clay and occasionally entire figures were constructed from thrown pots.

After World War II, a revival of interest in earthenware production techniques centred mainly on the colourful peasant wares indigenous to the Mediterranean area. White opaque and coloured glazes were used over the traditional red earthenware body. Decoration often recalled the work of the painter and included painted incised or modelled figures, sometimes rendered in an abstract style, sometimes more literally. When Picasso started to work with clay as a decorative method, either by shaping pots thrown to his direction on the wheel or by painting on them, such interest was shown in pottery as an art form that entire villages became full of potters making earthenware pots. Sometimes such bowls and dishes served a useful purpose but more often they were purely decorative and presented as works of art. This decorative aspect of French pottery reflecting the strong influence of fine art continues, and the pleasing and permanent effects which pottery offers have even induced painters to turn their hand to pottery.

Apart from the revival of earthenware a second major development has taken place in the last twenty years. In the centre of France in a district around La Borne a group of potters has existed for almost 400 years producing stonewares. The local grey clay is easily dug, highly plastic, almost free of impurities and withstands high stoneware temperatures. Thick forests surround the area and from the trees felled to provide brandy and wine casks, wooden off-cuts have provided and still provide cheap, efficient fuel both for large communal kilns and smaller private ones. Traditional wheel made forms, simple and strong in shape, all fulfilled a domestic need. Glazes, used sparingly, were simply made from equal proportions of clay and wood ash, although some potters also used

68

salt in the kilns for glazing. Each village or commune developed individual styles.

Five years ago only a handful of traditional potters were still working, but now the area has attracted a large and ever growing group of potters. What was becoming a neglected craft is again a thriving local industry to which potters came from many parts of the world. Hildegund Schlichenmaier (59), for example, is of German origin. Gwyn Hanssen (63) set up her workshop near La Borne some eight years ago after working in Australia and in Britain.

Some potters set up small workshops with several assistants and make basic functional wares related in shape to the traditional pots, and fired with wood and salt to achieve rich surface qualities. Other potters, attracted by a freer interpretation of traditional forms, produce lively and humorous but often useless wares. Recently, a third group can be identified, concerned more with the qualities of the clay and the wood and salt firings, and making sculptural objects which explore these qualities. Other potters collaborate with architects to produce tiles and murals for swimming baths and other such public buildings.

A particular feature of contemporary French ceramics is the absence of any great influence from the East. This is in strong contrast to Britain, for example, where Bernard Leach introduced this element in the twenties. Few potters in France were interested in Leach's ideas and many rejected them as belonging to another culture and to another age. They were more interested in looking at traditional and contemporary pots in France and other continental countries.

Large art schools with well established ceramic courses exist in the major cities throughout France, providing a wide variety of courses. As in other parts of the continent, trade fairs are popular occasions for potters to display work for the many craft shops throughout the country. However, unlike some European countries, there is no large, single association for potters, though the government helps craftsmen in various ways. French potters give the impression of working very much alone or in small related groups and do not feel the need or desire for such an organization. However the list of potters in a booklet entitled *Guide des Artisans et Créateurs de France* by Gilbert Delahaye lists many French potters and shows how widespread and popular the craft is today.

Vallauris, the pottery town in the South of France where Picasso first worked with clay, now organizes a large and impressive biennial international exhibition of contemporary pottery. The award of substantial monetary prizes is one indication of the respect given to the work of the potter.

In Holland artist potters have been working since the last part of the nineteenth century and the interest which started then has continued. One of the first Dutch artist potters, Lambertus Nienhuis, who died in 1956, had a beautiful studio by the canal-side in Amsterdam and this was taken over in 1958 by Jan de Rooden and his wife Johnny Rolf, two of Holland's leading modern potters.

Jan de Rooden (vii) makes a small quantity of domestic ware but the largest part of his work consists of objects and sculptures in which a single theme is explored over a range of pieces. Recent ideas have included the idea of 'pressure' and 'hard and soft'. In these pieces the use of stiff, solid, 'hard' areas is combined with folded, rounded, 'soft' areas. For the pot illustrated in colour plate IX, he has used handbuilding and thrown techniques. Johnny Rolf (68), uses more figurative subjects but she too will follow a theme, such as death or relationships, over a number of pieces. Both potters worked with reduced stoneware but now, conscious of the pollution such firings cause, limit themselves to stoneware fired in an electric kiln. Glaze ingredients are kept to a minimum often consisting of only two materials, with colouring oxides rubbed into the clay body. Both potters find stimulation in the traditional pottery of their own country, in that of the La Borne area of France and in English lead-glazed wares.

Other Dutch potters work in similar ways. Some like Adriana Baarspul (65) produced domestic wares but their main interest is in the sculptural object and, more often than not, one completely abstract in concept. Slab-built shapes which emphasize geometrical quality are often found in their work.

Unlike Holland, artist potters were slower to develop in Belgium, other crafts, such as jewelry and glass being favoured. However, during the twentieth century certain individuals have established for themselves an important role in studio pottery. Pierre Caille (70) who was born in 1912 and who has been working with ceramic sculpture since the late 1930s, has been chiefly interested in figurative work, sometimes of an almost unrecognizable kind, at other times of a symbolic force to convey a powerful psychological impression. He also uses birds and other animals in the same way, as if it is their effect rather than their resemblance to the original which is most important. Much of his work is given evocative titles such as *Melancholy Man*.

Carmen Dionyse (71) also works with figurative subjects and she too gives her pieces evocative titles, such as *Prophet with Hand* (1970) and *The Surprised* (69; 1971). Oliver Leloup is a young potter who has produced a wide range of humorous, bird-like creatures using earthenware and raku techniques.

Another of Belgium's young potters, Pierre Culot, trained at the Leach pottery in St. Ives, but rejected the style he learnt there and in his workshop designs and builds large decorative walls which explore the qualities of the clay rather than merely perfect a design concept. Recently he has produced large, substantial forms with ash glazes.

Emmanuel Cooper

London 1973

59 HILDEGUND SCHLICHENMAIER (France)
Vase 1972, stoneware body with brown and
grey sculptured surface, 21 in. Photograph by
Geremy Butler

60 ROBERT DEBLANDER (France)
Vessel 1972, stoneware body with grey and
brown flecked surface, 19½ in. Photograph by
Geremy Butler

France

59

60

61 EDOUARD SOLORZANO (France)
Jugs 1972, stoneware with ash glazes,
12 in.

62 Y. SEYVE and J. CHAUDET (France)
Vase 1972, porcelain, 6 in.

63 GWYN HANSSEN (France)
Lidded box 1971, porcelain, wood fired
kiln, 3 in.

64 JEAN TESSIER (France)
Pots 1972, stoneware, 24 in.

61

62

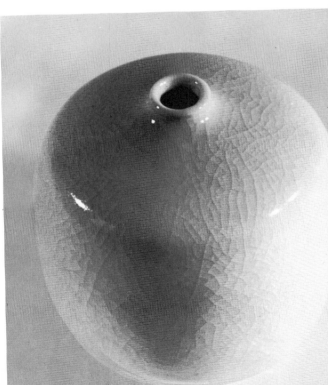

63

64

Holland

65 ADRIANA BAARSPUL (Holland)
Object 1972, stoneware with nepheline syenite glaze

66 HILBERT BOXEM (Holland)
Object 1973, stoneware with felspathic glaze, 10 in.

67 JAN VAN DER VAART (Holland)
Vase 1972, porcelain

68 JOHNNY ROLF (Holland)
Lidded box: 'Hibernation' 1972, stoneware with oxides over grogged body, bluish grey matt glaze, 9 in.

65
66

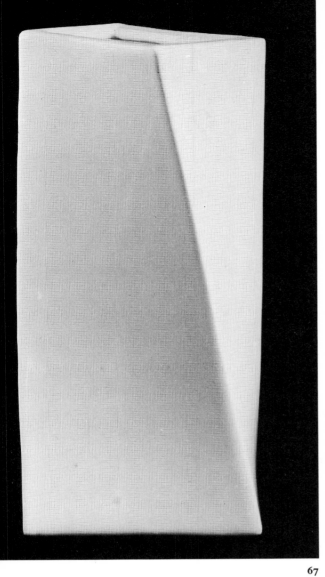

67   68

Belgium

69 OLIVIER LELOUP (Belgium)
'*Bird*' 1972, earthenware body with black and brown surface, 18 in. Photograph by Roland Lienart

70 PIERRE CAILLE (Belgium)
'*Cavalier*', stoneware, 12 in. Photograph by Yvon Caille

70

69

vii JAN DE ROODEN (Holland)
Composition with Sphere and Cube 1973, grogged
stoneware, length 15 in.

71 CARMEN DIONYSE (Belgium)
Sculpture 1972, stoneware with grey and brown glaze, 16 in.
Photograph by Carl Uytterhaegen

West Germany

One of the most important trends in the post-war development of ceramics is the movement away from functional use (which in Germany never quite reached the height of perfection obtained in England) to purely artistic aims. The increasing demands made by this departure from the protection of the functional market have produced an increasing number of young and talented artist craftsmen, who have overcome, with their new forms of expression, the supremacy of the thrown object. In spite of this, the thrown form, though almost declared redundant by some, has the vitality always to reassert itself, and some of the most worthwhile artistic results are obtained in this practical field. I would like, in this summary, not to follow a particular trend but to concentrate on the most important work. For this purpose I will take the contemporary artists in chronological order.

Hubert Griemert is the oldest of the potters whose work has its roots in the twenties and thirties. He continues to influence younger potters by his teaching. His thrown forms, distinctive and severe, are often decorated with fine crystal glazes (zinc silicate combined with barium and nickel) finely blended with the body. Margarethe Schott (75), a few years his junior, has been influenced by the Leach Pottery and developed highly fired reduction glazes to a new peak in Germany. She concentrates on a limited number of forms which her knowledge of glazes allows her to combine in new and exciting ways. She uses combinations of reduced iron and copper, often on a base of celadon, to get the glaze results which are of great importance. In total contrast stands the work of Walter Popp, who is nearly the same age as Margarethe Schott. In a singular way he has made pottery the medium of his subjective and highly charged personality. He uses large, often intersecting, glaze areas and strong brush decoration. He also uses built up shapes from thrown units, joined together in an angular manner, to express his style. His work includes sculptures and wall reliefs. The youngest members of this group are Ingeborg and Bruno Asshoff, whose work ranges wide. Their style is most easily recognized by the use of contrasting concepts in the same piece such as adopting a fragile and sensitive approach to archaic, simple shapes. Their range includes the thrown pot, the built and mounted shape, free construction sculpture and reliefs.

Among those born around 1930 there are two distinct groups: those who work in shapes based on the thrown pot and those who express themselves in the sculptural field. Among the former it is largely due to Karl (73) and Ursula (72) Scheid that the thrown pot, by its plastic richness and finish of form, might be the envy of a sculptor. Influenced by English stimuli they have found in reduced firings the right medium to make their stoneware or porcelain. Both Karl and Ursula make pure thrown shapes and Karl also uses shapes combined together from thrown or hand-built parts. Each creates a quantity of independent shapes which nevertheless form a mutual relationship and style of an

79

indissoluble unity which goes beyond the individual. This artistic unity is also enhanced by their mutual explorations and research into the realm of glazes and glaze control which is applied to both artists' ceramic shapes. The secret of their profound work is not so much that they are always inventing new shapes but they vary both the shape and glazing of their forms so that with a relatively confined number of basic shapes new facets are constantly discovered.

Görge Hohlt continued and intensified the work of his brother (who died young) with high temperature reduction firings but added to their range by introducing his own ash glazes. While Hohlt limits his work to the classical German shapes, Gotlind Weigel has enriched the types of thrown shapes both by reshaping standard ones and by adding a variety of entirely new forms, starting with the sphere. She has also developed exciting crystalline glazes and, lately, felspar glazes with her husband, who has added the winged vase to their range. Lotte Reimers (74) concentrates entirely on building up shapes from simple and rustic forms. She obtains her glazes from local stone and ashes.

In the plastic or sculptural group, Beate Kuhn (79) stands out. Her creations are composed entirely of thrown elements which she mounts together to create sculptural forms. This, combined with splendid glazes, is the key to her work. An inexhaustible imagination ranges from the monumental and very simple, to very complex structures including abstract and simple shapes that often display a sense of humour. Klaus Lehmann and Johannes Gebhardt (77) work mainly with wall reliefs. Lehmann works with finely shaped layers of clay which he glazes in black, brown or beige colourings. Gebhardt likes powerful structures reminiscent of geological formations with their crags, holes and outcrops. He also makes pure ceramic sculpture.

In the youngest age group, the inclination to a free, plastic form outweighs that of throwing or turning shapes without ruling out this type of ceramic altogether. Robert Sturm, originally a sculptor, cuts layers of clay and builds them up into shapes; Dieter Crumbiegel throws his components and mounts them; Horst Kerstan (76) concentrates mostly on typically oriental shapes but he also works in the abstract field under the influence of Arp, a series that commenced with his fruit pieces. A special and universally gifted artist among the younger group is Antje Brüggemann (80) who stands out equally with her thrown and built-up work. Her most original pieces include vases and still-lifes provoked by travels in Italy and Holland. While a new sentiment for realism seems to be pervading other artistic spheres at present, her work breathes the classical spirit and quiet tonality of Morandi's pictures rather than the hardness of the new realism.

Finally the contrast between two artists demonstrates the range of present-day work: on the one hand, Wolfgang Heynes with his strict constructions in sculpture and, on the other, Toni Heinrich (81), who draws his strength from an unusual imagination.

Paul Köster, Munchengladbach
translated by Henry W. Rothschild
1973

72 URSULA SCHEID
  Vase 1969, reduced porcelain with grey glaze and light
  border. Photograph by Claus Fulda

73 KARL SCHEID
  Pots 1972, stoneware. Collection of Boymans Museum,
  Rotterdam

72
73

81

74 LOTTE REIMERS
Vase 1972, stoneware, h. 10 in. Collection of
Princesshof, Leeuwarden

75 MARGARETHE SCHOTT
Vase 1972, reduced stoneware, iron and copper
oxide on celadon glaze. Photograph by Claus Fulda

76 HORST KERSTAN
Sculpture 1969, stoneware with spotted whitish
grey glaze, 9 in.

84

78

77 JOHANNES GEBHARDT
   Relief 1968, stoneware and fireclay with oxides, white
   grey cloudy glaze, 24 in.

78 ROBERT STURM
   '*Head*' 1969, stoneware, light brown glaze, 11 in.
   Photograph by L. Koster

79 BEATE KUHN
   Object 1972, stoneware, 12 in. Photograph by Claus
   Fulda

79

81

80 ANTJE BRUGGEMANN
Sculpture 1971, stoneware with whitish grey matt
glaze, length 13 in. Photograph by L. Koster

81 TONI HEINRICH
'*Cloudman on Rhino*' 1972, stoneware with grey and
brown glaze, 12 in.

Switzerland
Austria

The renewal of ceramic art in Switzerland is connected with the names of Mario Mascarin, Edouard Chapallaz (82), Philip Lambercy and Arnold Zahner, when they introduced stoneware into their country, under the particular influence of traditional Japanese ceramics. They are mainly concerned with research into giving form to objects of everyday use, and with the use of very rich glazes, which they frequently obtain through reduction in the kiln; an exception is Aerni-Langsch (84), whose work is devoted to the creation of large murals for public and private buildings.

The ceramic artists of Switzerland are associated in a 'Community of Work' which numbers about 200 members; its object is to maintain links among its adherents, to disseminate information and to organize exhibitions. The activity of this association stimulates museums and galleries to undertake a policy of information with regard to the public, in respect of research and development in the art in Switzerland. In the three important schools for the teaching of ceramic art, Berne, Geneva and Vevey, there are schools of applied art which have training periods of four years.

Nino Caruso

Rome 1973

In Austria an overwhelming influence on ceramics has come from the school of Applied Arts in Vienna. First brought into prominence by Michael Powolny, subsequent directors of the ceramics department have been Robert Obsieger and Heinz Leinfellner. Kurt Ohnsorg (1927–1970) the originator of the International Ceramics Symposiums studied there, as did Kurt and Gerda Spurey (85), two Viennese potters now working in an exploratory and creative way with porcelain.

Switzerland

82 EDOUARD CHAPALLAZ
(Switzerland)
Vase 1972, reduced stoneware, 18 in.

83 PETRA WEISS (Switzerland)
Vase 1972, stoneware with brown
and black glaze, 14 in. Photograph
by Peter Kopp

82

83

84 ELISABETH AERNI-LANGSCH (Switzerland)
Mural 1966, white earthenware. Photograph by
Felix Eidenbenz

Austria

85 KURT and GERDA SPUREY (Austria)
Torso 1972, porcelain, 22 in.

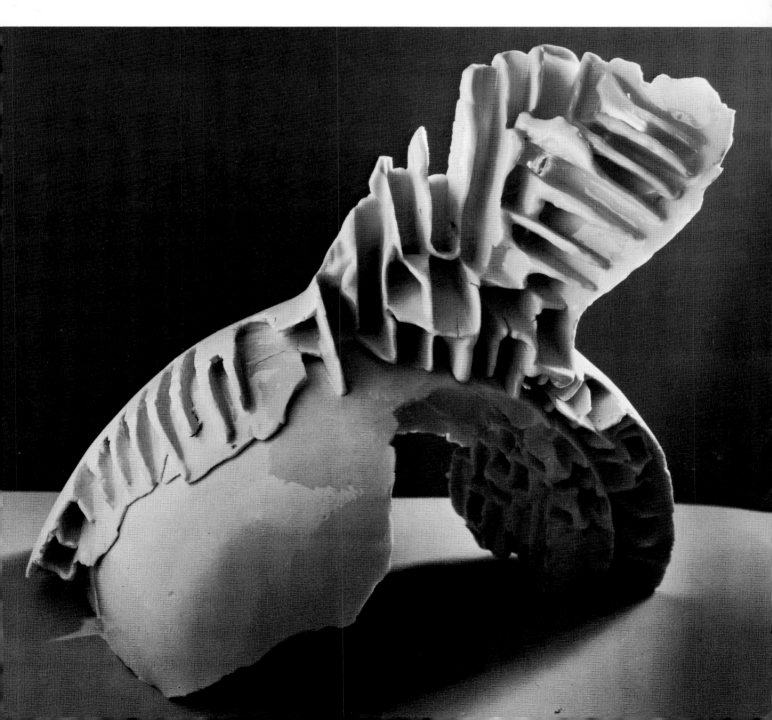

Italy
Spain
Portugal

Ceramic art in Italy, Spain and Portugal has a long history, well known and long since accepted as an integral part of every art connoisseur's cultural background. To understand recent and contemporary trends in this field close attention must be given to the period immediately following World War II.

The aftermath of the war brought with it a profound crisis in European ceramic art. The industrial and technological developments of that period were decisive factors in the rapid decline of those elements of cultural content which were still linked to tradition, and as a result craftsmanship, which had once constituted the vital core of ceramic art, became outmoded: at best it became identified with popular art; at worst it satisfied the tourist's demand for folklore. Industrial ceramics went through two stages of development: the first satisfied the demands created by reconstructing the economy of nations ravaged by war; the second had to meet the expanding requirements of a consumer society. This led to creative ceramics being confined within the ever narrowing limits of work done for special occasions or for an élite. To this must be added the influence of an official culture which is directed mainly towards the past, so that museums, periodicals and publishers in general concentrate on stimulating knowledge and investigation of the ceramics of the past, in the absence of any cultural policy for recognizing or supporting the work of today. The overall result is that the public knows almost nothing about what is at present going on in the field of creative ceramic art and is led through sheer inertia to attribute value to unimaginative repetition of outdated ideas and formulas.

This absence of any vital cultural policy has led to a kind of creeping asphyxiation in the field of creative ceramics, despite the fact that in the countries mentioned, and especially in Italy, there could exist, and indeed do exist, many schools to teach the art. In spite of this, there are groups of ceramic artists at work who have been trying to revive the art through years of personal dedication and individual research. They are guided principally by a desire to understand the relation between their activity and the world of today, and direct their research both towards using new materials and technologies, and towards freeing themselves from the traditional concepts which a romantic viewpoint had foisted on to the craftsman. At the present time numerous indications point to new cultural pressures acting on contemporary ceramics in each of the countries, though their results are not always homogeneous or comparable. There are many reasons for this, both historical and circumstantial, but common to all of them is the attempt being made to find a place for ceramics in contemporary culture. This leads to technological and technical experimentation with methods of work which differ from those of tradition, and which give rise to diverse aesthetic solutions. The tendency is to reintegrate ceramics into the real needs of present-day society, not as a fringe activity but within a more organic and coherent perspective.

In Italy the first attempts at a renewal were connected with the work of sculptors and painters, among whom Arturo Martini was one of the first. While he was working at Albisola (Savona) during the twenties, a succession of futurists worked at the kiln of Tullio d'Albisola, from Prampolini to Filli and Munari, producing ceramics with geometric stylization and complex works of striking vivacity of line.

Lucio Fontana, Agenore Fabbri and Aligi Sassu succeeded each other at Albisola. Fontana was without doubt one of the authentic and original masters of Italian ceramics, despite the fact that ceramics was not his constant concern. During this same period a group of master craftsmen was active at Faenza, including Melandri, Bucci, Biancini, and Melotti, who is well known for his very fine bowls, with their delicate, translucent colours.

Guido Gambone worked at Vietri sul Mare and later at Florence; Parini worked in Sicily and later on the mainland, where he became known for his ceramics in a popular style.

After World War II the sculptors Manzu and Garelli worked at Albisola, as did a group of foreign artists of the 'Cobra' group: Jorn, Appel, Corneille and Matta. Leoncillo Leonardi worked in Rome before the war, at first in a style associated with the Roman school, though distinguished by a certain expressionism; later, after going through a neo-cubist constructivist phase, he started informal experiments in which research into materials played an essential part.

The artists who today form the backbone of Italian ceramic art began working in the fifties. Despite various difficulties, such as the complete absence of a collectors' market in art ceramics and the above-mentioned lack of any cultural policy, they are successfully pushing forward the renewal of ceramic art, developing and refining its language within the social and cultural context of today, and at the same time incorporating a number of techniques which were previously exclusive to industry. Carlo Zauli (b. 1926) (87, 90) in Faenza, and Giovambattista Valentini (b. 1931) (93) in Milan were among the first to introduce stoneware into art ceramics.

New techniques are also being tried out. Alessio Tasca (b. 1931) (94) in Nove (Vicenza) uses a special process which allows him to create forms that go outside the tradition. I myself (viii; 89) often use collage and make modular forms with expanded polystyrene, which I model with a special machine. I am also introducing the concept of the module for the use of ceramics in architecture.

The archaic but extremely refined forms created by Candido Fior (86) are another new feature of Italian ceramics, and this striving for renewal is also to be seen in the large works of Franco Placidi (b. 1931) (88), with their sensitive modelling and decoration in monochrome slips and glazes. Finally we should mention the ceramic works of Gianfranco Trucchia (91) in Bologna, which recall pop art in the context of the expressive tendencies of contemporary sculpture; also the pure, functional forms, with their refined glazes, created by Franco Bucci (b. 1931) (92) in Pesaro.

The artists mentioned here belong to a very large group working independently in the principal regions of Italy. Very often their workshops are centres where young people can learn the craft; some of them teach in art institutes, of which there are twenty-five in Italy that teach ceramics. Among the most important institutes are those of Faenza, Rome, Bologna, Castelli, Gubbio, Deruta, Florence, Naples, Nove (Vicenza). In 1965 I established the International Centre for Ceramics in Rome, where ceramic artists from all countries meet in order to exchange experiences and gain new knowledge.

In Faenza, Gubbio and Vicenza national and international ceramic shows are organized annually. Some ceramic artists have also established effective links with industry, among them Pompeo Pianezzola and Franco Bucci. This enables them to introduce new concepts in the design of industrial ceramics such as those initiated some years ago by Gio Ponti and the firm of Richard Ginori.

The ceramic art scene in Spain today is marked by the presence of a number of younger artists, who are receptive to the new movements in aesthetics. Although they aim to express the restlessness of our time, these artists are aware of their responsibilities in regard to a glorious tradition. Los Serra, Elies, Aragay, Llorens Artigas and Cumella, to name a few, have given us works testifying to the revival which is common to nearly all European countries.

Llorens Artigas, who may be considered the pioneer of a new approach to ceramics in Catalonia, through his high temperature work, was influenced by the French attitudes of such men as Dufy and Braque. His work is pure ceramics, focussed essentially on the material, which he imbues with a purity of form and an extremely sober elegance. In 1959 he collaborated with Miró on some very successful murals. Antoni Cumella is another Catalan, whose originality is displayed in the tapering and egg-shaped forms he adopts, together with a colour scale of nordic tones. He specializes in stoneware work, which is almost unknown in Spain.

These two artists form a group apart from the young Spanish artists whose work is more strongly directed towards the world of today and the search for its significance. Among the most significant of this younger generation of artists are: Arcadio Blasco (b.1928); Elena Colmeiro (b.1931) (96); Ramon Carrete (b.1938); Enrique Mestre (b.1936) (95); Federico Ilario Giner (b.1936); Lluis Castaldo (b.1936); Pere Noguera La Bisbal; Elisenda Sala. Almost all of them were trained in the ceramic schools of their own country, of which the most important are: in Barcelona, Escuela Messana, Escuela del Trabajo, Escuela de Artes y Oficios Artisticos; in Madrid, Escuela de Ceramica, Escuela de Artes Applicadas y Oficios Artisticos; in Tarragona, Escuela de Artes y Oficios Artisticos; in Valencia, Escuela de Manisses. These schools are academic in aspiration except the Messana school in Barcelona, which has given up the traditional teaching system and turned its attention to the more advanced manifestations of contemporary ceramics.

It should also be pointed out that in recent years certain industrial centres have promoted the setting up of a Seminario de Estudios Ceramicos de Sargadelos in La Coruna, and the organization of ADI-FAD (Agrupament Disseny Industrial del Foment de les Artes Decoratives) in Barcelona. This centre for industrial design in ceramics is specially engaged in the design of ceramics, and in promoting training schemes so that ceramic artists can be employed in industry.

In Portugal, a fresh look at ceramics occurred in the fifties, owing in particular to the interest shown by a number of sculptors and painters in this ancient craft. The younger artists were the first to make contacts between their craft and contemporary culture, introducing new concepts and techniques into strongly traditional atmosphere in which ceramics had held a position of great prestige. Among them are Artur Jose, Lisbon; Maria Manuela Madureira, Lisbon (b. 1931); Mario Ferreira da Silva (97), Villa Nova de Gaia (b.1934); Maria de Lourdes Castro, Lisbon; Francisco Relogio (b.1926). The most important schools of ceramics are Academia di Belas Artes, Lisbon, Scula Antonio Arroio, Lisbon and Academia Belas Artes, Oporto.

Nino Caruso

Rome 1973

viii NINO CARUSO (Italy)
'*Sculpture Objects*' 1969, cast earthenware with
white and coloured glazes, 11 in.

Italy

86 CANDIDO FIOR (Italy)
'*Image 5*' 1972, terracotta, 2 in.

87 CARLO ZAULI (Italy)
'*Explosion*' 1972, stoneware with
white glaze, 6 in. Photograph by
Antonio Masotti

86

87

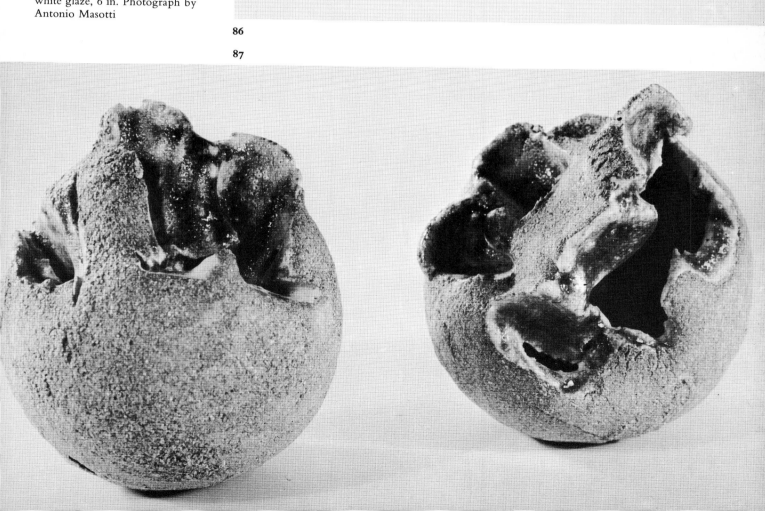

88 FRANCO PLACIDI (Italy)
  'White Great Image' 1968, earthenware body with white slip and glaze, 5 ft.

89 NINO CARUSO (Italy)
  Sculpture 1972, cast fireclay with matt white glaze, 5 ft.

89

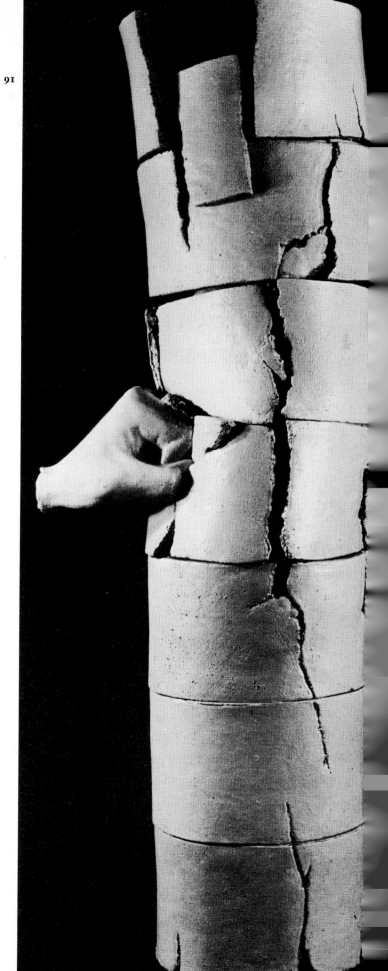

90 CARLO ZAULI (Italy)
  '*Horizontal Quiver*' 1972, high fired red clay
  with white/grey glaze, length 3 ft

91 GIANFRANCO TRUCCHIA (Italy)
  '*The Column*' 1970, stoneware with white
  glaze, 7 ft

92

93

92 FRANCO BUCCI (Italy)
'*Sculpture units*' 1972, stoneware with
white and black glazes, width 12 in.

93 GIOVAMBATTISTA VALENTINI
(Italy)
'*Totem*' 1972, stoneware with brown
and white glaze. Photograph by Bruno
Gecchelin

94 ALESSIO TASCA (Italy)
Coffee set 1972, earthenware, made
from extruded units, with white and
grey glaze

94

95 ENRIQUE MESTRE (Spain)
Sculpture 1972, reduced stoneware with
brown glaze, 2 ft.

96 ELENA COLMEIRO (Spain)
Sculpture 1972, stoneware with white, blue
and black glazes. Photograph by Fernando
Nuno

Portugal

97 MARIO FERREIRA DA SILVA (Portugal)
   Sculpture 1972, earthenware body with grey glaze

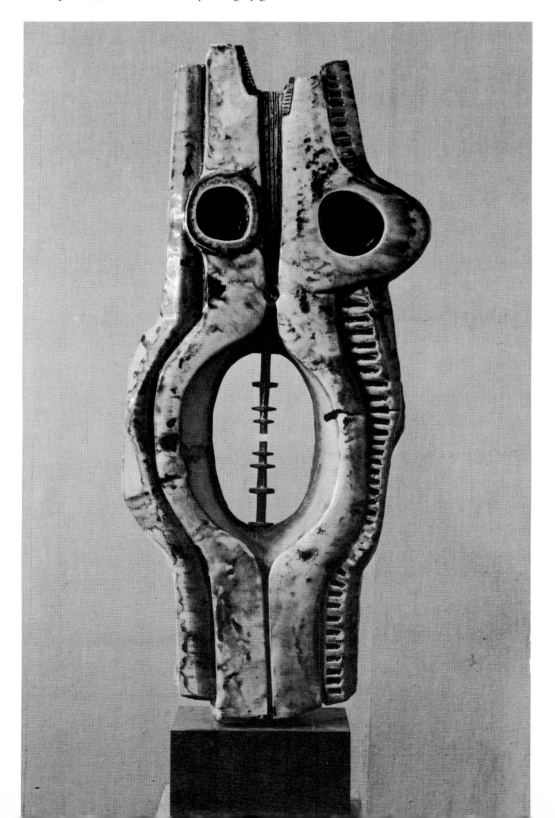

Bulgaria
Hungary
Yugoslavia
Poland
East Germany
Romania
USSR

To assess the present state of ceramics in these countries, it is necessary to consider their history. Bordering as they do the ancient civilizations of Asia, their territory witnessed one of the oldest neolithic cultures in Europe. Then, in addition to the indigenous population, many migrating peoples have left behind them traces of distant cultures. While in western Europe a favourable climate gradually developed for the emergence of national civilizations, whose progress was checked only occasionally by local conflicts, and north-east Europe was enjoying a comparatively calm period, in the south-east the indigenous population, both then and in the later Byzantine Era, was to be in a state of discord for a thousand years, firstly because of a continuous influx of alien peoples, and later because of the Turkish occupation which endangered the identity of the original inhabitants.

The formation of present-day Hungary, Yugoslavia, Bulgaria, Poland, Romania, as well as parts of the USSR, was thus achieved over a longer period than was necessary for the formation of the different nationalities in western Europe. One of the results of this has been that the pottery of eastern Europe is very diverse in character, while current archaeological excavations continue to reveal even more varieties of ware. For the same reasons a wide range of popular pottery has continued down to our own times. There are still centres in Romania where tens, or even hundreds, of peasant families carry on traditions which are as old as they are diverse, for example the pottery of Marginea, near Suceava in Northern Moldavia, or Hurez, which continues a Byzantine tradition similar to that of Bulgaria. The pottery of Vadul Crisului, which is also in Romania, continues the Roman tradition and there are many other examples. In Transylvania, as a result of the coexistence for several hundred years of the Romanian population with others of Hungarian or German descent, areas can still be found where the pottery has preserved a greater purity of

105

character than that found in its original centres, where such traditions were destroyed long ago by industrialization.

Among the east European countries considered, the widest variety of peasant pottery and continuity of traditional forms can most easily be found in Romania and in the regions of the USSR. Bulgaria, with a much smaller population, provides only a limited selection. Popular ceramics is still alive in these countries, partly because of late industrialization, and partly because of the custom of honouring the dead by offerings of new earthenware bowls, a tradition unknown to the Roman Catholic peoples of Hungary, Poland and Czechoslovakia, and to the Mohamedan minorities of Yugoslavia.

It is also significant that none of these peoples ever had a tradition of making porcelain or stoneware, or in any use of high temperatures. Working either with common ferruginous clay or with white clays, the peasant craftsmen of these countries use primitive, wood-burning kilns, often sunk into the ground. They decorate the pots, which are mostly bowls and jugs, either with coloured slips, under lead glazes, or by burnishing the unfired pot with a stone. This simple method of decoration, which originated in antiquity, is still practised in Northern Moldavia and Southern Poland on black or red pottery, and such work continues to be made at Sacel in the Maramures, Romania.

The small but flourishing tradition in functional ware in Bulgaria, Yugoslavia, Romania and some areas of the USSR may account for a certain lack of interest in it on the part of trained ceramists. They are more interested in sculptural ceramics, whether they derive their inspiration from Stone Age forms or current international trends. By contrast in Hungary, Czechoslovakia and Poland, functional ware does interest the educated potter, either because of a nostalgia for folk art in the case of the Hungarians, or, in the case of the Poles, because of an interest in stoneware, under the Leach-Hamada influence, this interest went hand in hand with designing for industrial mass-production.

This state of things, conditioned by the social circumstances of these countries, is currently undergoing a new development. Naturally it varies from country to country and depends partly on the education and training available, partly on the emergence of outstanding individual artists. After World War II such artists as these drew the attention of the young generation to the wider horizons now opened to them by ceramics.

Factors in all these socialist countries ensure pottery a major place among the arts, while in western Europe it is still common for cultured people to consider ceramics a minor art form. Both the laws of the state and the organizations for the arts protect and give certain rights to ceramic artists, in exactly the same way as to their colleagues in the pictorial, sculptural and graphic arts. Under these conditions, the only competition the artists have to face is in trying to improve the quality of their work and in introducing new ideas. Here, ceramic craftsmen do not run the risk of being crushed by 'business' or compelled to restrict their inspiration for fear of giving away their secrets. In a sense, they might be working within an overprotective situation with a consequent loss of initiative, but that remains to be seen.

A second factor contributing to the progress of ceramics in these countries is the support artists receive from the ceramic industry. Production in ceramic factories in Romania, for instance, has increased tenfold in the last few years, making it possible each year for many potters to work in industry alongside the permanently employed designers. It is not only that the factories possess the necessary technical knowledge, which is not easily acquired in a country with no tradition of high temperature firing, but this technological background has enabled them to explore the possibilities of clay as a creative material in directions previously unimaginable. This is regardless of whether they are working on one of a kind pieces or models for mass-production.

Recent innovations in architectural design, such as the building of prefabricated, standardized housing, use fired clay products to enliven exterior surfaces. Ceramics are also used in large factories, art centres, theatres and new towns where they can help to produce a more amenable visual environment. This has encouraged many young artists and has resulted in an increased appreciation of ceramics as an art form. It can also help satisfy the spiritual needs of the community, and act as an antidote to the cold sterility of so much of the industrially produced landscape.

Since the educational systems in all these countries are different, there is no tendency towards uniformity in their cultural life. Again, art education is sensitive to the needs of society and this is reflected in the relationship between the number of students trained and the work available to them on the completion of their courses. In Romania, for instance, most young ceramists leave university with an almost fully developed individual style and are well able both to deal with the problems of working for industry, and to produce the original pieces needed for decorating public buildings and their surroundings.

National and International Symposiums are also an important aspect. They help to give the ceramic object, apart from its function of individual usefulness, a new collective function, that of a social art needed to enhance the environment.

An aware and well-informed society is undoubtedly necessary to the development of the creative capacity of any artist today. Ceramists can avail themselves, along with all other artists, of the very useful information facilities provided by the cultural exchanges among these countries, such as scholarships and information tours. In addition, for two years now, Romania has organized national symposiums in which about twenty to thirty young ceramists meet, discuss and pool their experience. The Hamangia Foundation, an offshoot of the Union of Fine Arts of Romania, has a specially equipped house on the Black Sea shore where it sponsors symposiums. In the next few years these will become international.

Following the examples of Austria and Czechoslovakia, such international symposiums have been arranged in recent years in Hungary and the USSR. It is largely as a result of them that changes can be seen in the ceramic art in these countries. Many of the ceramists who have had the opportunity of such contacts were already qualified artists, but others, younger and less experienced, have shown a quite remarkable development. The symposiums also have the merit of bringing life to the entire community where they are held. As such they are true festivals of pottery, modern ceremonies open to the entire population of the small towns where they take place. They fulfil a positive function in the education of the community and deserve the envy of the other arts.

Only a limited number of ceramists may truly be called artists. Only the very best, those who by their exploration of fundamental ideas really attain new levels, can be considered, and they are still very few. A large majority of potters continue to be satisfied with established formulae. Yet the most important thing in the development of a culture is a favourable climate for creation, and the present activity in the socialist countries should produce an impressive progress of ceramic art.

Patriciu Mateescu

Bucharest 1973

98 IVAN NENOV (Bulgaria)
Sculpture 1972

99 ANTONINA KONZOVA (Bulgaria)
Decorative panel and objects 1972

100 OLIA KOLTCHEVA (Bulgaria)
Sculpture 1972

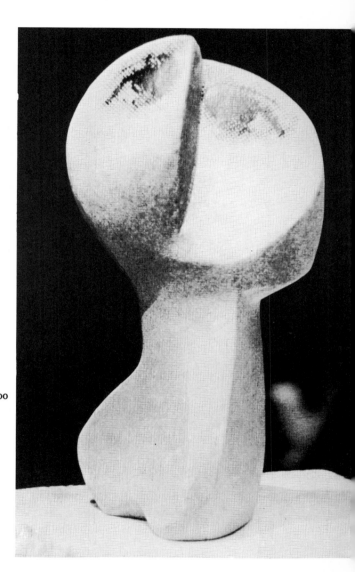

Bulgaria

98

99

100

109

Hungary

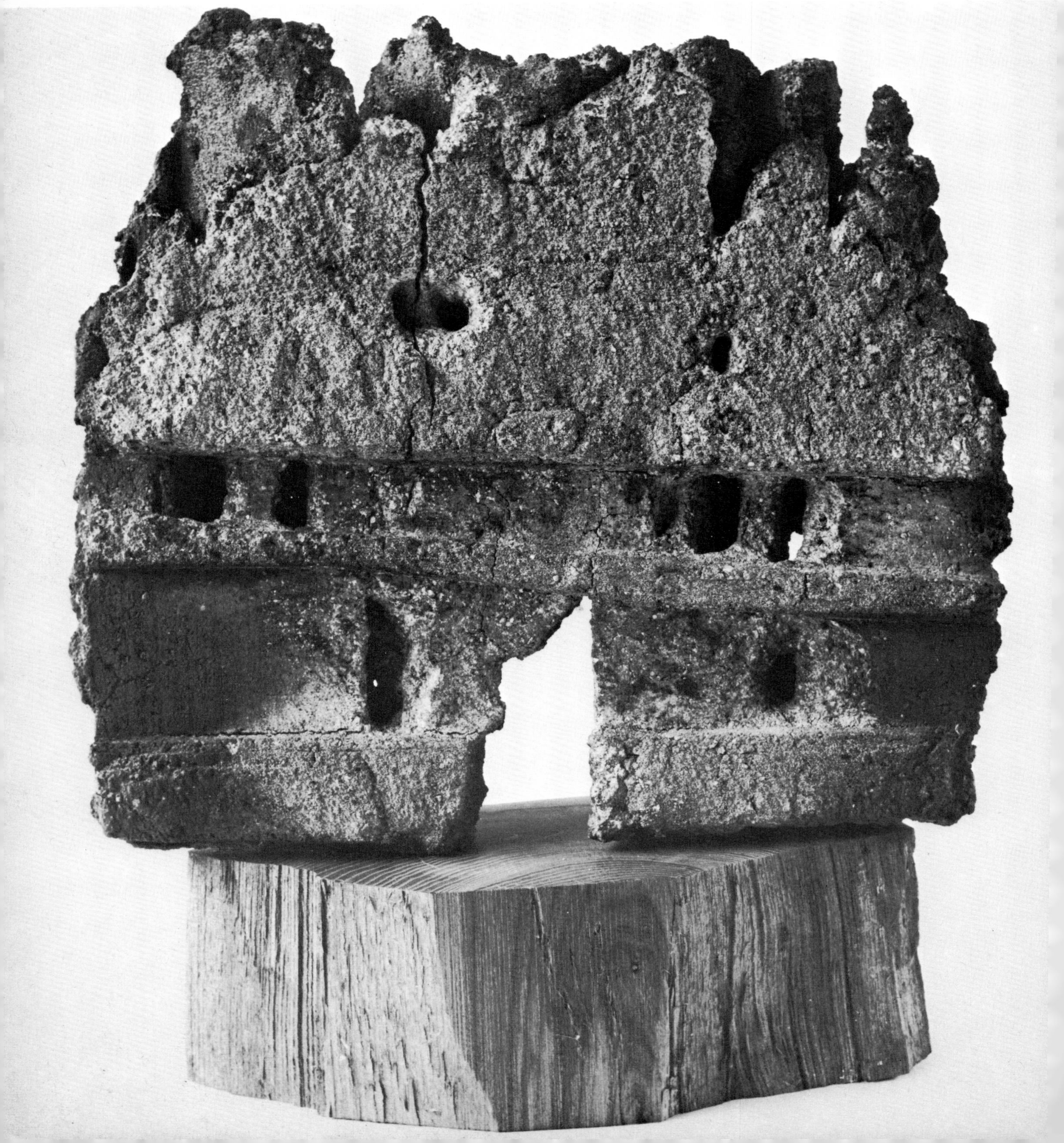

101 IMRE SCHRAMMEL (Hungary)
'*Old Castle*' 1972, stoneware body with
black and brown surface, set on wooden
base, 19½ in. Photograph by Geremy Butler

102 IMRE SCHRAMMEL (Hungary)
Mural detail, unglazed terracotta, 12 ft × 28 ft.
Budapest Historical Museum

103 VLADIMIR KUCINA (Yugoslavia)
Don Quixote and Sancho Panza

103

102

Yugoslavia

104

104 HANIBAL SALVARO (Yugoslavia)
Vases

Poland

105 ELZBIETA EWA MEHL (Poland)
Bird 1972, 24 in.

106 EDWARD ROGUSZCZAK (Poland)
Dish 1972, width 28 in.

105

106

East Germany

107 BARBARA LOFFLER (East Germany)
'*Frau en der soffa*' 1971, 16 in.

108 WALTER GEBAUER (East Germany)
Pot, about 6 in.

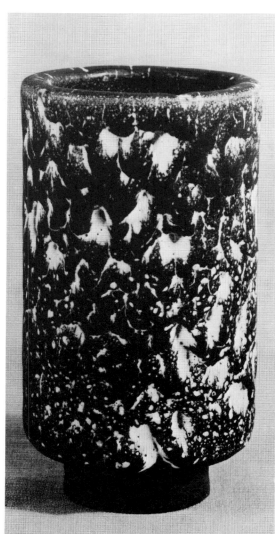

Romania

109

109 PATRICIU MATEESCU (Romania)
'*S.24*' 1972, biscuit porcelain, 24 in.

110 ILIE BELDEAN (Romania)
'*Efervescenta*' 1972, 20 in.

110

114

III

112

111 VICTOR CRISTEA (Romania)
'*Arbore*' 1972

112 IOANA STEPANOV (Romania)
'*Raising*' 1972, stoneware, 9 ft.

113 COSTEL BADEA (Romania)
'Contrast Mineral' 1972, matt glaze

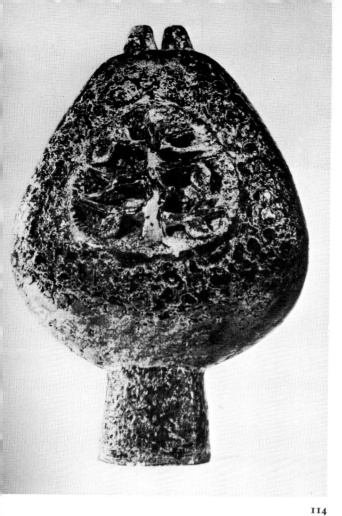

USSR

115

114

114 TARAS POROZNIAK (USSR)
Sculpture 1972, 26 in.

115 VERONIKA OREHOVA (USSR)
Sculpture 1972, 18 in.

116

117

116 PETER MARTINSOH (USSR)
Sculpture 1972 15 in.

117 MAIA KOOLBERG (USSR)
Two pots with ornate handles 1972

118 GRAJINA DEGUTITE (USSR)
Pots 1972 11 in.

119 FIRA GREKU (USSR)
Tall objects 1972 5 ft.

120 GENOVEITE JACENAITE (USSR)
Figure 1972, 12 in.

118

119   120

Czechoslovakia

Studio pottery is firmly established in Czechoslovakia today and owes much to the teaching of Helena Johnova, who was appointed Professor of Ceramic Art at the Prague School of Applied Arts in 1919 and who had been a pupil of Michael Powolny in Vienna. One of her most notable pupils, Otto Eckert, is the present Professor of Ceramics in Prague. This generation of potters was strongly influenced by the teachings of the Bauhaus on form and reacted strongly against what appeared at the time to be the overdecorated 'Art Nouveau' style of earlier Czech artist potters. Since 1945 this somewhat austere attitude has given way to a freer and often more imaginative approach, and work has been produced that is closely related in feeling to painting and sculpture. In particular one would mention the reliefs of Antonin Bartos (122) and the sculptures of Josef Susienka (121).

Potters working in Czechoslovakia today are fortunate in that ceramics are widely used in conjunction with architecture. Murals are often required for the exteriors and interiors of public buildings, and special individual pieces are commissioned for architectural settings. Lydia Hladikova, Devana Mirova and Marie Rychlikova are three potters who share a studio in Prague and work mainly with architects (123). Although there is plenty of opportunity for potters to design for the tableware industry, most ceramists seem to combine these activities with working on individual pieces. Pravoslav Rada is well known for his humorous majolica pieces (126) and Lubor Tehnik has recently experimented with porcelain, using this traditionally delicate and controlled medium in a free expressive manner (125).

Czechoslovakia has been prominent in sponsoring the working International Symposiums which have been held almost annually since 1966, and a special Museum of Contemporary Ceramics has been established in the small pottery town of Bechyne in Southern Bohemia to house a selection of pieces from each symposium. Apart from the foreign participants the symposiums are attended both by well-established and younger, less experienced Czech potters and are proving a useful source of stimulation. Of the younger ceramists the work of Vaclav Serak should be noted (127).

Eileen Lewenstein

London 1973

121 JOZEF SUSIENKA
Garden sculpture '*Multiply*' 1972, white glazed stoneware, width 16 in.

122

123

122 ANTONIN BARTOS
Relief 1971, porcelain, 24 in. × 17 in.

123 LYDIA HLADIKOVA, DEVANA MIROVA,
MARIE RYCHLIKOVA
Decorative panel 1971, for trading house in Hradec
Kralove, five standard tiles, 10 in. × 10 in.

124 ALENA KROUPOVA
Stoneware vases 13 in.

125 LUBOR TEHNIK
Goblet 1971, porcelain, 12 in.

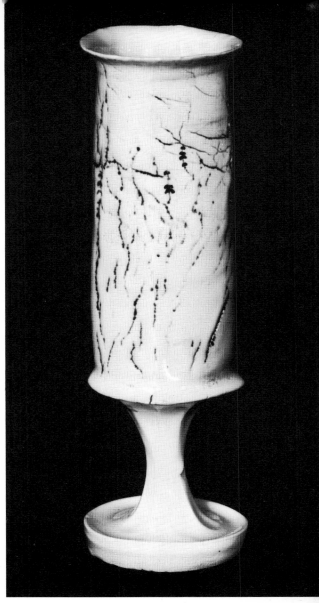

125

124

123

126

124

126 PRAVOSLAV RADA
   'Lady with Flower' 1971, majolica, 18 in.

127 VACLAV SERAK
   Relief vase 1972, stoneware body
   with blue, white and buff glaze,
   30½ in.

127

Greece

Some sixty years ago, at Amarasion about ten miles outside Athens, individual potters discovered the remarkable qualities of the local clay and since then the area has attracted potters from many parts of the world. A wide range of work is produced which varies in style from imitation antique Greek black and red wares to the finest hand-built porcelain. Most pots are thrown on the wheel and fired to earthenware temperature.

Valsamakis is the oldest and one of the most respected potters in Amarasion. About ninety per cent of his work consists of large tile murals, mostly for government buildings. Many other potters produce such murals, for example, Vernadaki, the wife of an architect who first studied in Britain. She now has her own shop in Athens where she sells her pots and decorative tiles. A younger potter, Jota Melion, in her early twenties learnt pottery from her father and is already establishing a name for herself. She too produces murals and pots, drawing inspiration from the traditional pieces of Ancient Greece.

In contrast, Mary Chatzinikoli works in Athens with porcelain. She makes her organic, rounded forms by hand-building methods and achieves an almost paper-thin quality in her pieces. Maria Voyatzoglou, also working in Athens, produces tile panels and individual pieces (128).

128 MARIA VOYATZOGLOU (Greece)
  'Flat Ceramic Surface' 1972

Turkey

Two factors are at work in modern ceramics. The International Ceramic exhibitions and competitions held in various countries are having a wide effect, promoting both the exchange of ideas and criticisms of ceramic art today. Secondly, towards the end of the nineteenth century ceramic arts in the West were belittled by the term 'minor art', and even today the classical Fine Art Academies have not abandoned this concept; only painting and sculpture are considered 'major arts'. But it cannot be denied that after World War II, the great painters and sculptors who worked with ceramic material brought to it a greater value in terms of shape and colour.

Turkey is a country that has emerged from the deep-rooted civilizations of Anatolia. The ceramics found at Catal Huyuk (7000 BC) can be described as sculptural in terms of shape, painterly in terms of colour and functional in terms of use, and thus embody an expression of the highest value. These ceramics continue to be a subject for study by archeologists throughout the world; some pieces were shaped into the first sculptures made by human hands and some were pots made of baked earth, found near the kitchens of the houses; they were perhaps the very first clay articles made for everyday use.

The study of contemporary Anatolian folk pottery has been very enlightening for us, and has been particularly helpful in training young potters. Traditional methods are well-established within the community being handed down from father to son or from master to apprentice. The boys start working during the long summer holidays while they are still attending elementary school. If they cannot find employment locally they will then travel to work with relatives who have pottery workshops elsewhere in Anatolia, or even as far away as Istanbul.

The Ceramic Arts and Industry High Training Schools and also the ceramic section of the State Academy of Fine Arts, which I founded in 1930, provide for ceramics to be studied both by potential designers for industry and by ceramic artists. Recently a talented group of young artists has emerged.

It has been difficult for contemporary Turkish ceramic art, which has characteristics differing from those of other countries in the West, to break away from classical traditions and become western oriented. Until World War II, the ceramic exhibitions organized in this country could not compete with the developments and progress achieved in other branches of art. However, in the years 1930 to 1942 the seeds were sown in the field of ceramic art, and after 1942 collective and individual ceramic exhibitions have been important steps that have paved the way to present-day work.

Contemporary ceramic art has come to be recognized in other countries through their participation in the exhibitions organized by the International Academy of Ceramics. The Academy has arranged exhibitions in Cannes (1954), Ostend (1959), Prague (1962), Geneva (1965), Istanbul (1967), London (1972) and Calgary, Canada (1973). These exhibitions have been important for ceramic artists in Turkey and have helped to continue discussions on the meaning and purpose of ceramics as an art form today. We know that clay is a material which can be used as creatively as any other. Its art value, aside from all prejudices, depends on the character and individual expression of the artist. The end product can be a masterpiece of art.

Ismail H. Oygar

Istanbul, 1973

129 ISMAIL OYGAR (Turkey)
Relief panel 1972

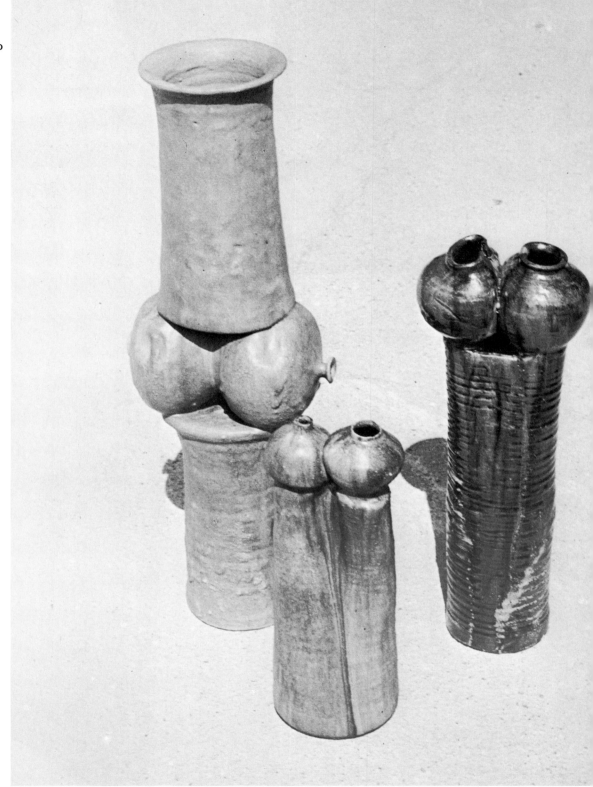

Israel

A large and thriving group of potters work in Israel and exhibit many influences in their various styles. Perhaps the majority of the work is sculptural rather than functional, such objects being constructed by almost any available technique, including coiling and throwing. Some of the work reflects a concern for and involvement in contemporary events, for example, the work of Agi Yoeli (134). Much sculptural work is used to decorate the exterior surfaces of buildings as well as the inside walls of houses and offices. Functional work is usually thrown on the wheel, and both earthenware and stoneware temperatures are used.

An active organization for potters is the Ceramic Artists Association of Israel at Tel-Aviv, which is concerned with conveying information and arranging exhibitions. It acts as a central liaison point for potters who wish to show work overseas and generally promotes the work of the studio potter.

130 FILIZ OZGUVEN (Turkey)
Pots 1972

131 HANNA CHARAG-ZUNTZ
(Israel)
Bottle, blue and black terra
sigillata, 12 in.; *Liquor set and
bottle*, stoneware, 8 in.

132 LYDIA ZAVADSKY (Israel)
Relief 1972, 28 in. × 18 in.

133 EDITH ADY (Israel)
Object 1972, stoneware, 28 in.

134 AGI YOELI (Israel)
'*Astronaut with Cat*' 1972, 32 in.

133

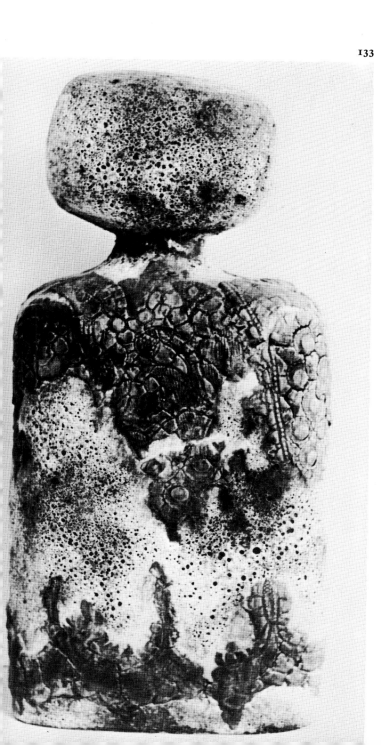

134

135 NAOMI BITTER and NORA KOCHAVI (Israel)
'*Mirage*' 1972, 43 in. × 21 in.

134

136 GEDULA OGEN (Israel)
    '*Sabra Cactus and Thorns*', detail of mural, earthenware, 6 ft × 15 ft

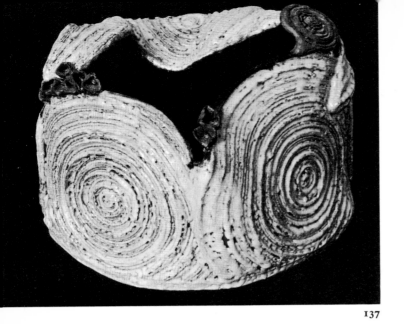

137 GINA ROTEM (Israel)
Vase 1972, stoneware, light grey glaze outside, black
inside, width 11 in.

138 SHELLY HARARI (Israel)
'Jerusalem Hills' 1972, detail, earthenware with
engobes, diameter of whole sculpture 9 ft.

137

138

Africa

South Africa is the most active centre for ceramics in Africa. Immediately after World War II a few potters started working here and have now grown into a thriving and expanding group. A particular feature of South African ceramics is the making of murals and wall decorations for public and private buildings, an activity encouraged by an adventurous approach on the part of young architects. The size of many of these murals offer a great challenge to the potters.

One of the oldest and largest pottery workshops is that belonging to Sammy Liebermann who started working some nineteen years ago after training at the Chelsea pottery in London where he handled earthenware techniques. In his first workshop Liebermann employed only one assistant, but today he has at least nine throwers who make functional earthenware. He is also helped by his wife who does tile painting and murals.

A native influence on many South African artists was provided by the painter and art historian Walter Batiss when he wrote a book on the artefacts and wall paintings of the Bushman of the Kalahari desert. Potters as well as painters incorporated in their work the motifs of the Bushman, and one such potter, Esias Bosch, started his pottery career making earthenware decorated with Bushman motifs. At his workshop at White River, Eastern Transvaal, he now makes reduced stoneware, digging his own clay and prospecting his own raw materials. As well as producing a range of domestic wares he undertakes commissions for murals for public buildings, for example, a very large relief mural for the Jan Smuts airport, Johannesburg. Bosch has just started to work with salt glaze. Tim Morris, a potter trained in Britain, works in Johannesburg producing reduced stoneware very much in the Leach tradition.

Johannesburg art school has a sizeable ceramics department, where studio techniques and some industrial techniques are taught. Other art schools with ceramic departments are at Capetown, notably the Michaelais Art School associated with Capetown University, and at Durban.

South African potters are currently in the process of forming a potters association very much on the lines of the Craftsmen Potters Association of Great Britain, to be known as the Association of Potters of Southern Africa. The interest shown in its formation reflects the professional and general interest in pottery, both as a full-time and a leisure time activity.

Native African pots are still made in North Transvaal and Natal but demand and supply is lessening as western culture makes their use obsolete. Two notable attempts are being made to teach the black Africans how to produce studio pottery, one in Swaziland and one in Lesotho. Both workshops receive financial support from government or industry and both aim to employ and train black Africans. Professional potters run the workshops which produce tableware in reduced stoneware.

Sculptural objects are made by a few potters, but such work does not yet

137

command a large following. Pieter Maritzberg, a friend and student of Liebermann, makes ceramic objects. Andrew Walford, another younger potter specializing in more individual pieces, trained in England and visited Scandinavian and Japanese potters before setting up his workshop in South Africa.

Rhodesia is, in many respects, similar to South Africa except that less work is produced. There are few full-time professional potters, and they concentrate on domestic ware. The University at Salisbury has no art department, but art schools in other parts of the country have small ceramic centres. On the whole, the preference in exhibitions is for traditional thrown tablewares; ceramic objects are still viewed with a degree of suspicion by selectors and organizers. African pottery continues to be made in traditional ways in Matabeleland and Mashonaland.

In Nigeria several notable attempts have been made to found studio workshops. First Harry Davis and then Michael Cardew went from Britain to set up pottery workshops. The venture not only involved training unskilled black Africans, but also prospecting and mining suitable clays and raw materials. The low temperature, traditional African red and brown earthenware, was considered unsuitable for use in contemporary life, though the making skills, strong shapes and lively decoration were greatly admired. One of the aims of the workshops was to preserve these skills so that many traditional shapes were incorporated in the range of reduced stonewares.

Two potters from Zaria, Isaac Olusegun Aina (139) and Saidu Na' Allah have made interesting attempts to integrate traditional shapes into their own work. Using the technique of reduced stoneware, in many ways their pots merge the essence of the African and Western cultures creatively. They are a promising development for the future.

139 a and b

139 a & b ISAAC OLUSEGUN AINA (Nigeria)
Flower vases 1971, stoneware body with pink and brown glaze, 10 in. and 6 in. Photograph by Geremy Butler

140 ALICE HEYSTEK (South Africa)
Pot 1969, stoneware, textured surface, 14 in.

140

India

Studio potters work in many diverse ways. Some have trained in the East, particularly in Japan, others have studied in Britain, either at art schools or in workshops. The work of Indian potters in general reflects this broad training, though some, such as Satish Gujral (145), have become very concerned with the traditional motifs of Indian art and have used them in their work. The large mural, of which a part is illustrated (143), is an excellent example.

The Indian Studio Potters Association in Bombay keeps its members in touch with each other and also organizes exhibitions of their work. Primula Pandit (141), the secretary of the association, is one of India's best known potters. She makes both sculptural objects and wall decorations for which she uses porcelain with impressed and art decoration. Vimoo Sanghri (144) has a studio in Bombay. After training in Britain he now makes individual pots in earthenware, some with matt rough surfaces.

141 PRIMULA PANDIT (India)
Sculpture 1971, white porcelain with copper wire decoration, on a rosewood base, 16½ in.
Photograph by Geremy Butler

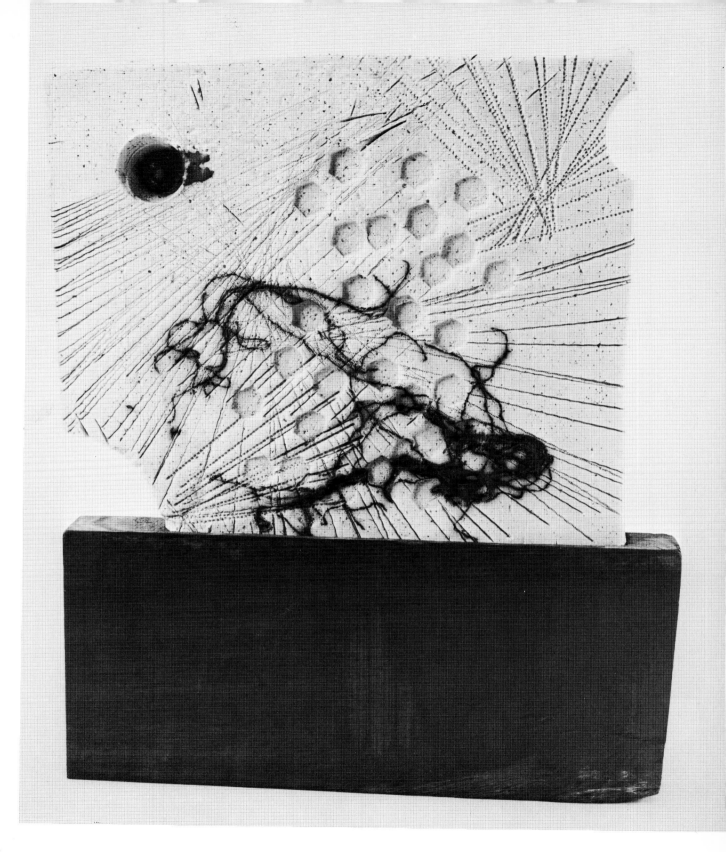

143

142

142 SATISH GUJRAL (India)
Ceramic mural 1968, detail

143 GURUCHARAN SINGH (India)
Vase 1972, stoneware with white slip, 12 in.
Photograph by Indergrewal

144 VIMOO SANGHRI (India)
Pot 1971, earthenware body with brown and
cream glazes, 9 in. Photograph by Geremy Butler

145 SATISH GUJRAL (India)
Sculpture, length 13 ft

144

145

Canada

Canada stretches for more than three thousand miles from the Atlantic Ocean on the east coast to the Pacific Ocean on the west. There are three main regions, the West, Ontario and Quebec, and the Maritimes, yet more than half of Canada's 22 million inhabitants live in two of Canada's ten provinces, namely Ontario and Quebec. Canadians come from many diverse ethnic backgrounds, and are influenced by different elements depending on the area of the country in which they live, for the prevailing cultural influences in each area exhibit both similarities and distinct differences. Naturally, these are reflected in the arts. There is also an outside influence on artists in Canada, namely international trends, particularly those from England and the United States. It is not possible to illustrate every facet of current activity but potters who are exploring new fields will be mentioned even if space does not permit a fuller discussion of their work.

Until about five years ago most potters in Canada were making functional wares, but today it is the ceramic object-makers who are more predominant. Objects are being produced, shown and collected, so that an increasing number of people are gradually coming to enjoy, even if they do not fully understand, this new work. Right across the country, potters, now usually known as ceramists, are making things which one would not normally expect to find made of clay; stoves, cricket boxes, grocery stores, food, boots, coke cartons, satchels, figures and so on. Super-realism as well as changes in scale often prevail in many of the pieces, but it is also evident that the objects are not quite what they appear. Bits of feathers, pieces of fur, leather lacing, metal fastenings, paper cloth and almost anything else is employed to further an idea. Bright colours, lustres, and low fired white clays are employed and seem to lend themselves to the sculptural use to which they are being put.

David Toresdahl of Surrey, British Columbia, works in this way, often adding feathers, hair and gold leaf to his fired objects, for example his *Ceremonial Nightstick* (147). In the western area of Canada, particularly in British Columbia, there is a strong influence from the United States. In Alberta, which has almost acquired a tradition of innovation, it is now the 'primitive' potters and object-makers who are best known. Mary Borgstrom who lives in a rural area of Alberta, has led many people to an interest in primitive pottery, and Gillian Hodge has worked throughout the west on her natural and earthy approach to ceramic art. Ann Marie Schmid-Esler (150) makes beautiful porcelain beds and pillows, which convey well a feeling of lightness and fluffiness. Harlan House (152, 156) produces model cars with distinct personalities. In Saskatchewan, the Californian influence seems most pronounced amongst the object-makers and the three prominent ceramists are Marilyn Levine, who did her graduate work in California and is now back working in Regina, Saskatchewan, Joe Fafard (146), whose ceramic figures have great immediacy, and Victor Cicansky who

ix LUCIA TEODORESCU (Romania)
 'Decorative Form', 24 in.

makes humorous pieces. New work began to develop in Manitoba in 1970, and one notable artist is Stanley Taniwa (153) who exhibited a pot-bellied stoneware stove in the fall of 1972 at the Winnipeg Art Gallery.

Since more than one third of Canada's population live in Ontario, naturally this province is a hive of activity. Toronto is a sophisticated city with many art buyers, and though the recent trends in object-making did not originate here, they have certainly attracted the interest of ceramists. Consequently, such work is successfully made, exhibited and sold. Potters such as Angela Fina, who has done a lot of experimental decoration using photographic processes on pots, Mary Keepax (154), whose spheres and egg-like porcelain environments are superbly well-made, and David Gilhooly (148) can find a ready market for their work. Gilhooly, who came from California via Regina, brought with him his particular ceramic sense of humour and is now influencing potters here as much as he did in the west. His work can only be described, unpromisingly, as part of the frog world, yet he manages to make not only appealing but engrossing social comment. Made from his own particular blend of white clays with a little bit of pearlite added he has what he considers a perfect base for his colourful low fire glazes. Georget Cournoyer of Montreal, Quebec, has recently been winning international awards with her carefully made, hand-built stoneware bags and sacks in natural earth-like colours which, by their realism, have an eerie quality.

The ceramic department at the Nova Scotia College of Art, Halifax, under the direction of Homer Lord and Walter Ostrom (149), is having a notable influence on ceramics on the eastern seaboard. So strong is this influence that students are transferring from universities in Canada and the United States to do graduate work at this college. The department is innovative and energetic, artists are invited from far and wide for short visits at the school, and Exhibitions are held in which staff and students show work. The result is that people in the area are becoming more aware of the non-functional possibilities of ceramic art. The most interesting event to come out of the school this past year is AWAL T 26 – the name of a computer programme originated by Ostrom, which makes possible the tabulating of all glazes in the cone 8 to 10 range, and calculates there to be 11,125 theoretically possible glazes. Anyone in the world who has access to a computer is free to regenerate the programme, which has been picked up in other parts of North America and in Europe. This exciting and useful exchange of ceramic information is available to potters regardless of language. It is art information documented and communicated, ceramic information not visual, but visualized. This abstract information potters can transform into reality.

Schools and educational opportunities for ceramists in Canada continue to play a vital role in the development of the art. Fifteen years ago it was almost impossible to get a good education in this field. Today there are institutions across the whole country where a student can be well trained in the technical, practical aspects, and where his aesthetic sense and creative abilities will be encouraged. Many ceramic colleges now have a glass workshop where students can work as part of the curriculum. Most schools also operate summer programmes for a shorter term. On these courses freer, more exploratory working methods are encouraged. Raku, smoke firing, open pit fires and the use of natural clays are all methods which allow the ceramist to get away from the well-equipped studio and use instead ingenuity and skills with simple materials.

In 1972 a student ceramic show, in which most of the colleges that offer ceramics took part, revealed definite trends and influences. On the whole young potters were making objects and sculptures full of social comment, using clay, not as an end in itself, but as a medium for expression. Differences could be detected from school to school, but new trends were apparent nationally.

One other new direction should be mentioned, namely there is a growing frequency amongst young potters to set up studio potteries. Many of these studios are partnerships operated by couples who have just graduated from ceramic colleges or trained through apprenticeships with established potters. These studios often concentrate on functional ware and meet with gratifying success, as more people buy hand-made pots.

A common thread links potters across the land. Ceramic art in Canada has been built on a foundation of traditional functional work which has grown increasingly in quality year by year, and is still growing. In the seventies, however one can see new trends emerging in which both young and not so young potters are involved. Two main areas, whose finished products contrast markedly, stand out, both involving experiment, both involving the concept of 'getting your head into it'. The first is primitive pottery-making, using simple direct methods, and represents a movement to a more natural way of doing things; the second is one in which ceramic expression is characterized by an awareness of the culture in which we live. Through ceramics views of contemporary culture are expressed, which are often topical and often satirical. Although social comment is not new in art, in North America at this time ceramic art does strike certain notes with which the viewing public can identify. Because of interest shown by schools, sound art training, and increasing support by the government and the public, it is now possible to earn your living being creatively involved with pots. Finally, Canadian ceramics are very definitely influenced by world trends. Obviously, as North Americans, we interact with our fellow ceramists in the United States yet, even so, a close study of the work reveals a subtle difference, a distinctive Canadian style and direction.

Gwen Sands

Toronto 1973

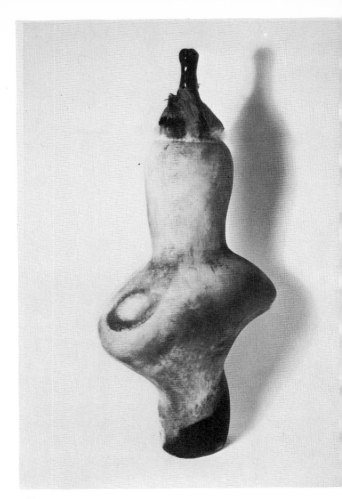

146 JOE FAFARD
Figure 1971, earthenware body, brightly
glazed, about 7 in.

147 DAVID TORESDAHL
'*Ceremonial Nightstick*' 1972, 32 in.
Photograph by Lynn Vardeman

148 DAVID GILHOOLY
'*Frog Fred*' 1973

149 WALTER OSTROM
Lidded jars 1972, saltglaze, 15 in.

150 ANN MARIE SCHMID-ESLER
Lunar Loaf No. **1**' 1972, stoneware with
black lustre glaze

146

149

150

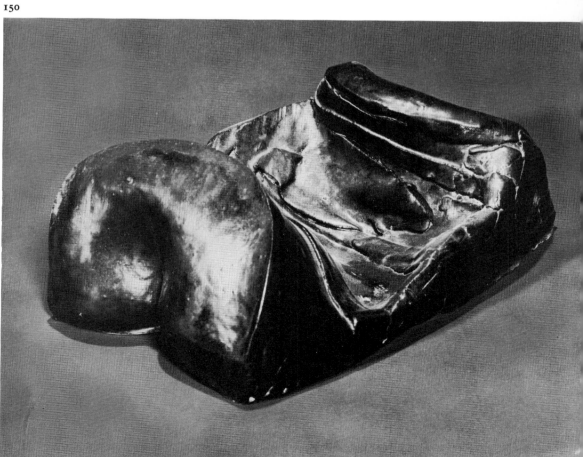

151 JOHN CHALKE
  Left: *Pot* 1971, stoneware, thrown and
  assembled with lustre and agate glaze

151a PIERRE GUY
  Below: *Sculpture* 1971, unglazed stoneware with
  incised decoration

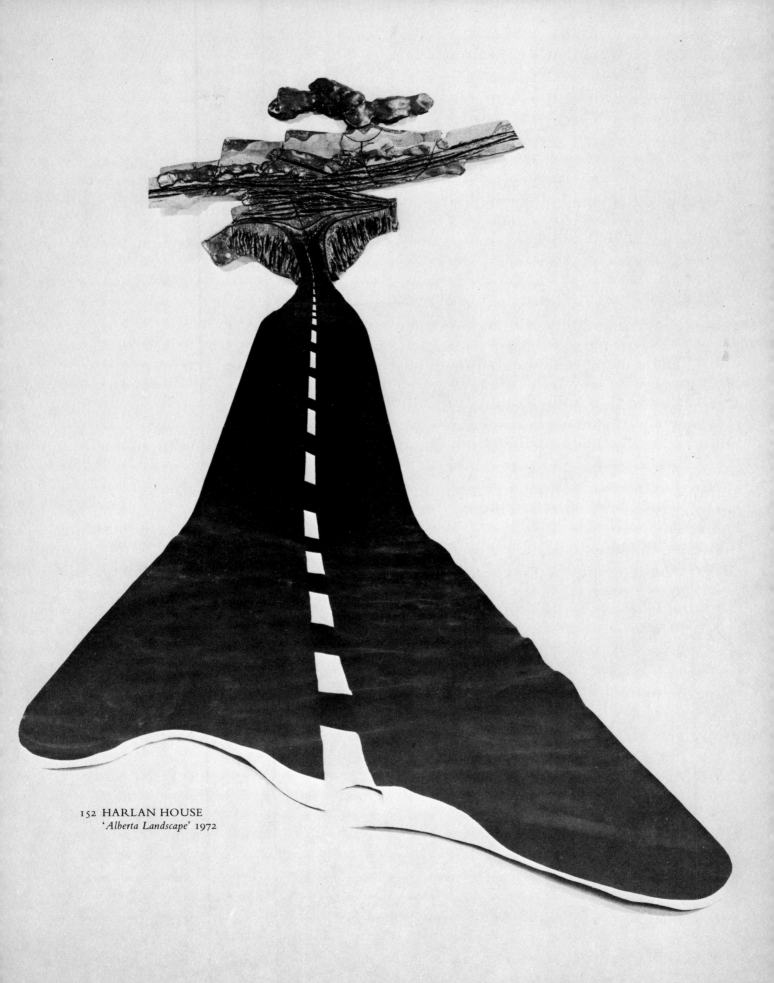

152 HARLAN HOUSE
'*Alberta Landscape*' 1972

153 STANLEY TANIWA
'Pot Bellied Stove' 1972, stoneware, 37½ in. Photograph by Ernest Mayer

154 MARY KEEPAX
Egg forms 1972, oxidized porcelain with fawn matt textured glaze, 3½ in. and 2 in. Photograph by Geremy Butler

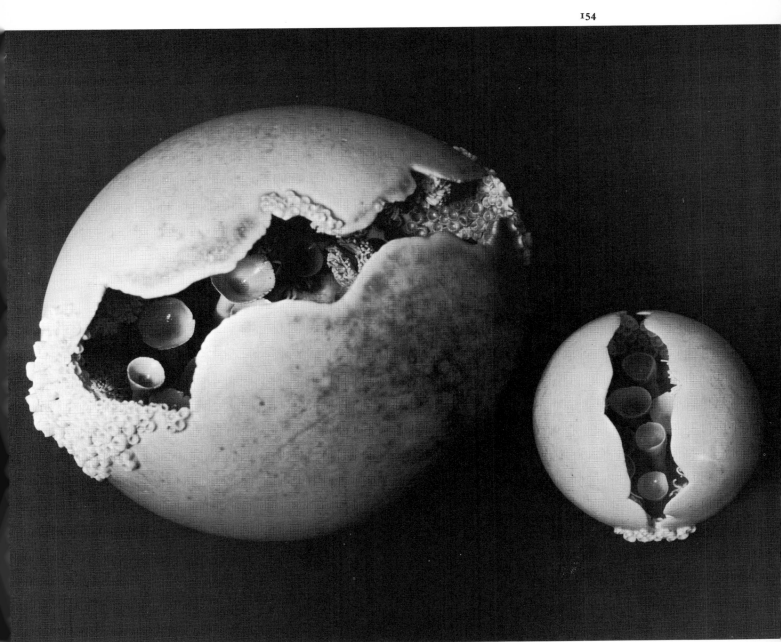

155 RON ROY
Covered jar 1971, earthenware body with white raku glaze, 5 in. Photograph by Geremy Butler

156 HARLAN HOUSE
'*1946 Sports Special*' 1972, length 15 in.

155

156

United States of America

In order to gain an intelligible insight into the contemporary ceramics scene in the United States, it is necessary to divide the work into three or four loosely defined categories. These divisions are somewhat arbitrary, in that most of the work does not belong exclusively in any one category, but, to gain some understanding of the diversity of attitudes that exist, it is helpful to recognize that a number of distinctive form-concepts have been established.

Probably the majority of ceramic work being produced today in America falls into the area of wheel-thrown, utilitarian pottery. This is natural enough, since America's varied ceramic heritage has developed from pottery vessels made on the wheel, displaying frequently the complex symmetry of Graeco-Roman forms and the more simplified and somewhat informal balances of the Orient. A casual survey of work seen in shops, galleries and studios who deal primarily in utilitarian wares shows a wide variety of shapes, decorations, glazes and methods of execution. Although most of the work made on the wheel has a similarity of form, strong identities are often retained by personal approaches to decorating and glazing. Frequently potters resort to the smallest idiosyncracy, such as a different way of treating a rim or foot, or the application of slip or glaze, in order to give their work a personal stamp. Varying approaches to handling wet clay on the wheel further enhance the wide repertoire of form-concepts that are found within the limits of utilitarian pottery. It can vary from spontaneous and vigorous throwing, shown by the prominence of finger ridges, to an exactitude of finish that often resembles slip-cast ware.

Until quite recently, the romanticism and 'mystery' of reduction-fired stoneware was predominant. Traditional oriental glazes such as iron-saturated browns, opaque and transparent celadons, stony matts, wood ash and slip glazes were among the most popular. Pseudo-oriental approaches to decoration often contrasted with more precise, geometrical patterns. Recently salt-glazing has emerged as a rival to these other, more established approaches to finishing pottery. Inventive use of slips and engobes, fuming with chlorides and the introduction of various organic materials such as rubber, leather or manure into the kiln at the time of salting has created a new sense of excitement among both production and studio potters who deal with more individual problems.

It is difficult to estimate how many potters are earning their livelihood from making and selling their own work, but, in the last five to ten years, increasing numbers have faced the problem of using their skills to establish production lines, most of the products of which are sold from their own studios. It is equally difficult to estimate how many shops or galleries are selling hand-made ceramics, however, in comparison to ten years ago, more outlets are now available to potters who wish to sell their items by established wholesale or retail methods.

Equally popular as the production of utilitarian pottery is the making of more decorative wares. Here, the potter frees himself from the exclusive utilitarian considerations of such items as pitchers, teapots, casseroles or mugs, concerning himself, instead, with the idea of creating an object whose main function may be nothing more than that of ornament. At times this can allow the potter more liberty to 'experiment', both in terms of shape and decoration.

Many potters who work in this more decorative way seem to be preoccupied with embellishing the surfaces of pottery vessels. Interestingly the most extensive surface decoration occurs on relatively simple, classical shapes, a favourite form being the closed, ovoid bottle shape. Traditional techniques include crystalline glazes, lustres, underglaze, overglaze, wax resist, sgraffito, enamel overlays and ceramic decals. Innumerable methods of making textures are continually explored in order to create rich, sumptuous sensations, both tactile and visual. Appendages, and the inclusion of foreign materials such as wood, metals or fabrics have also become an integral part of the vocabulary of the ceramic artists who believe that a piece of pottery can, in fact, become a 'picture-in-the-round'.

Potters have always decorated their wares in one way or another, history being resplendent with fine examples. Some contemporary ceramic artists, however, investigate decorative possibilities, not to complement the basic form, nor to reinforce the basic structure, but rather to create subtle tensions between the shape and the decorative motifs, whether they are figurative or not. It is therefore not unusual to find relatively basic forms given heightened expressive potential by the use of highly ornate decoration.

This sort of romanticizing about the surfaces of pottery vessels has led to further exploration of the shape itself. If, after all, this attitude towards decoration were followed to its logical conclusion, further obliteration of the surface would lead towards alteration of the structure. As a result of this tendency there has built up gradually a body of work that could be loosely identified as 'bent ware', or transitional ware, transitional because it occupies a peculiarly ambiguous position between the traditional pottery vessel, which is clearly identified with the symmetry of the wheel, and that of the more sculptural, asymmetrical, free-standing ceramic form.

Although much of this work is initially created on the wheel, it is often subjected to slight alterations by padding, pushing, denting, gouging, cutting or making additions. These actions are prompted not so much by a desire for novelty or merely to be different but by attempts to create new or more personal relationships between the artist and his product. The innate characteristics of the soft, pliable clay container are considered as a starting-point for further exploration. Rather than remain within what some potters may feel to be the constraints of the wheel, the imposed symmetry is used as a point of departure so that, in a sense, the wheel is merely a useful tool to create numerous forms that can be altered in a variety of ways at a later stage.

An attitude of improvisation has also fostered sympathies towards more sculptural considerations among American artists. All ceramics are sculptural forms, merely because of their three-dimensional nature, but the artist working in clay has to determine whether to satisfy utilitarian needs or to aim for a full sculptural entity, devoid of utility. The impression that American ceramics consists only of sculptural types of work is not correct, as a large amount of exquisite utilitarian work is being made and is comparable to any produced in history, yet it is the sculptural work that has gained more attention from critics and teachers because it seems to be endowed with a new sense of adventure and modernism.

Because of the complexity of attitudes to this kind of work, further sub-divisions will help. Abstract Expressionist painting and sculpture have provided an important catalyst for the ceramic artist who wants to introduce a quality of suspended animation into his work. The intensity of pushing, cutting, hammering or tearing the clay are often effects which give this type of work an energy seldom otherwise seen, although what may appear to be a haphazard juxtaposition of slabs of clay may actually be a very well thought out, but quickly executed, statement. To work in this manner almost requires that the artist does not approach his object-building with a precise, clear, preconceived notion of what will happen. Changes occur during the actual making which can bring forth lively relationships of colour, texture, line, shadow, voids and planes not clearly identified at the outset of the creative act. What may appear to be unresolved visual relationships are actually deliberate efforts to realize a quite opposite notion that there must always be a foot and a rim, a beginning and an end.

Out of these attitudes has come a re-definition of craftsmanship. Whereas in the past (and especially with regard to utilitarian wares) craftsmanship was equated with exactness and precision, ceramics which uphold an Expressionist philosophy foster a more direct and more spontaneous way of handling materials and tools. Because a piece of work has an 'unfinished' or coarsely constructed look about it, this does not necessarily indicate an insensitivity or lack of skill on the part of the potter who created it. Instead, it is part of the total emotive impact.

Working on a large scale has become another important preoccupation for many American ceramists. Although welded steel sculpture has probably had some effect here, the American environment is perhaps equally influential with its mammoth scale in highways, buildings and vast open plains. Cavernous exhibition spaces in which to show work has also affected the ceramic artist's competitive spirit. Now that ceramists have overcome the technical problems of building huge forms and the kilns in which to fire them, it is not unusual to find ceramic forms of six to eight or ten feet tall. It is not proposed that scale for its own sake is the main criteria in this work, merely that some ideas are difficult to express on a small scale. In a country where visual perception is conditioned by extremes, it seems natural that this is reflected in contemporary ceramics.

Philosophical considerations of conceptual art and surrealism, as they relate to painting, sculpture and psychology, continue to have a strong impact on contemporary sculptural ceramics. In addition to the more conventional and traditional techniques of creating clay objects, numerous decorative approaches are being resurrected which, in the past, were essentially outside the domain of pottery. Slip casting, press moulding and throwing are being supplemented by decorative methods such as ceramic stencils, photo-silkscreening, underglaze drawing pencils, china paints, metallic lustres and even non-ceramic paints.

These techniques are used in the most personal, highly mysterious and symbolic way yet to appear on the American ceramic scene. The final visual statement often adheres to a kind of classic simplicity and orderliness, yet the literal and surreal associations created by juxtaposing fragmented images often border on the occult, the bizarre, the absurd and the whimsical. Since these artistic works have few discernible clues as to their literal interpretation, one is often left wondering whether they have meaning for anyone other than the person who created them. Such work has found enthusiastic support among the younger, more recently graduated students of ceramics.

Perhaps no other expression in contemporary American ceramics has aroused more interest, both negatively and positively, than that which embraces the aims of Pop art. Of major interest are ideas containing some sort of social commentary, whether it be on some historical/religious event such as the Last Supper, or the political hysteria surrounding the American involvement in Vietnam. Not all the chosen subject-matter is so ponderous, however, and many artists are able to make some comment on themselves and their world in a more lighthearted way. Emotionally charged symbols, such as the stars and stripes, bombs and peace emblems, as well as cars, food, words and slogans, are all part of the basic vocabulary of ceramic artists who find it important to express their feelings and ideas about the *status quo*. In addition to the use of literal images, the inclusion of crude colours and garish, metallic surfaces help to formulate a complex iconography that grows out of and reflects the American scene.

Funk art owes much of its popularity to ceramics. In this case, an amazing array of ceramic and non-ceramic materials and techniques are used to arouse every sybaritic nerve. Some artists work in relatively abstract terms and allow the natural quality of the soft, oozing, sensual clay to stimulate a wide variety of emotions. Among the more provoking statements are those that resort to the explicit use of erotic images. The phallus, breast, mouth or tongue are among favourite symbols used to comment on the Puritan ethic and lampoon many deep-seated psychological enigmas. No theme remains inviolable to the ceramic artist who is intent upon salacious commentary. No technique, either of construction or decoration, seems to have escaped the probing sensibilities of artists dedicated to the idea of giving form to what some people feel are the neuroses and preoccupations of the psyche of many Americans. Of course, Funk art lends itself to numerous interpretations, and the degree to which it is refined often determines whether or not it becomes a sensitive, intelligent ennunciation or merely remains a statement of crass insensibility. Both qualities are plentiful in American ceramics today.

Often in the past the skills of the painter or draftsman were utilized in order to enrich the potter's work. Nowadays, not only are the painter and potter one, but potters are often also trained in various two-dimensional processes. Many potters have been able to synthesize these skills and create for themselves highly personal statements, both in form and decoration. Interestingly enough, of these techniques, all but perhaps photography are used in rather traditional ways. What sets these efforts clearly apart, however, is their content and the context within which they are used.

In some instances obvious references are made to the minimal and hard-edge painting which has been popular in America for the last ten years. In stark contrast to this is a return to a more academic modelling of recognizable subject matter, usually within the framework of the pop, funk, conceptual and surrealist considerations. Equipment such as the airbrush, which previously has been a mainstay of commercial artists, has become increasingly popular with ceramists. This has resulted in some of the most sensitive drawing ever to appear on American ceramics.

Many artists working in clay never seem to be satisfied with the mastery of a particular technique or idea and relentlessly push beyond 'acceptable' norms. For example, they will use acrylics, enamels, phosphorous paints, automobile laquers and even housepaints. These potters discard the idea that ceramics should become part of a heritage Some even take their work no further than its fragile, raw stage, so that when it is subjected to the elements of nature such as snow, rain, wind and frost, it will in time disintegrate. It is almost as if the artists who produce these forms are asking themselves, 'Why, after all, should a work of art, created from a piece of clay, be any more enduring and precious than a human life?' This may not be a philosophical proposition so much as reflect the American belief in obsolescence.

Every work of art is in some degree experimental. But there is one area within the ceramic arts that is undergoing a change that appears to be peculiarly American. Some current work incorporates plastics, metals, fabrics, glass and neon lights, so that clay almost plays a subordinate role. The inclusion of transistorized sounds has added yet another dimension. Of all explorations, these seem to be the least resolved, but with time and experience, some fascinating ideas will probably emerge.

It would therefore seem that no one particular 'style' or philosophy prevails in contemporary American ceramics. There continues to be a wide proliferation of techniques and ideas which co-exist, sometimes perhaps uneasily. In the eyes of the sensitive teacher and artist, both attitudes (the conservative or traditional on the one hand, and the avant-garde or experimental on the other) depend and feed upon each other, rather than cancel each other out. The contrasts provide opportunities for each artist to reassert a commitment to his particular expression.

But what about the American ceramic artist and his relationship to society? What, if any, is his role, and how does he 'fit' in? There are at least 450 colleges and universities or art museum schools that teach ceramics. Seventy-eight of these have graduate programmes which supposedly prepare one for a career in ceramics, many of them promoting the idea that it is more important to develop self-expression than to reach a high level of technical proficiency. There are probably not more than a half-dozen schools that specialize in training young people specifically as production potters, though there are production potters making very respectable incomes from their work, which is viewed with genuine respect by their colleagues, young and old. However, in relation to the number of ceramic artists who are working on a one-of-a-kind, exhibition basis, production potters in America are relatively few. In an affluent country such as this, why are there not more potters committed to producing their own ceramics commercially?

Generally, American art schools do not have courses similar to those found in Europe. Nor are there any apprenticeship systems. With few exceptions, students in American universities are trained to become teachers in high schools and colleges where they may perhaps become 'artists-in-residence'. Although this system may be viewed with some misgiving, one cannot deny its substantial results, since most of the best ceramic work in this country is made by artists who are also teaching. So one of the main reasons more potters are not earning their livelihood exclusively from the sale of their own work is because, in part, they have not found it necessary to do so.

Any real relationship between the American ceramic artists and industry is almost totally non-existent. Except in rare instances, American potters are not trained to work in the problem-solving situations found in industry. At the same time, industry has shown no particular interest in doing anything other than perpetuating the same designs that have proved successful for the past twenty-five to fifty years. Suspicions on both sides have stood in the way of bringing about a healthy exchange between the creative forces of artists and the productive possibilities of industry. This may change if the public demands better, more imaginatively designed products and if industry recognizes this. A wider world market of competition may also force American industry and artists to combine their efforts in order to improve the current low standard of design. Until this happens, or until the individual production studios become a more attractive means of earning a living, the majority of American ceramic artists will continue to produce objects dedicated to establishing their own creative expressions.

Paul S. Donhauser

Wisconsin, USA 1973

157 KAREN KARNES
Lidded jar 1973, saltglaze, 20 in.

158

158 RICHARD PEELER (Peeler Pottery)
Domestic pieces 1973, stoneware

159 CURTIS HOARD
'Childrens Landscape' 1972, white
earthenware clay, low fire glaze, 12 in.

159

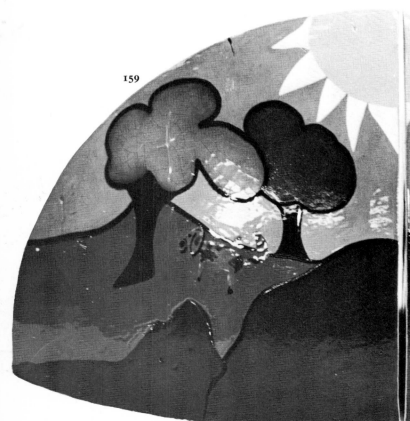

160 HUI KA KWONG
  Objects 1972, white earthenware
  with overglaze decoration, 10 in.

161 KENNETH VAVREK
  '*Air Cooled Tangerine*' 1972

x PATTI BAUER (U.S.A.)
'*Car Kiln*' 1972, length 36 in.

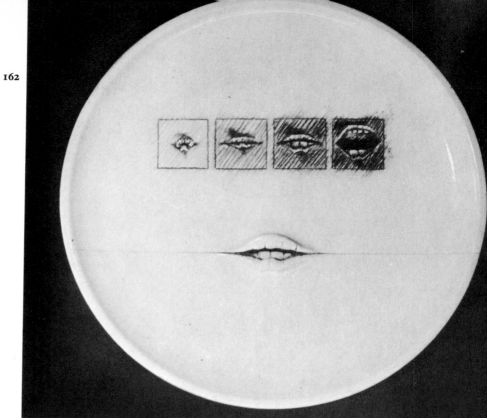

162

162 VERNE FUNK
'*Four stages of mouth*' 1972, earthenware
with underglaze pencil decoration,
width 15 in.

163 SUSAN HALE KEMENYFFY
Platter 1972, raku, width 24 in.

163

164 HENRY K. GERNHARD
   'Wishing Well' 1972, 18 in.

165 BILL FARRELL
   Vase 1972, stoneware, slab-built, 36 in.

166 JIM STEPHENSON
   'Clay Horn' series 1972, 18 in.

164   165

166

167 PAUL DONHAUSER
Pot 1972, saltglaze

168 WARREN MACKENZIE
Four vases for a gynaecologists office 1972
porcelain, 6 in.

169 PAULA WINOKUR
Wedding pot 1972, hand-built porcelain, lace
impressed design with a clear glaze, 22 in.

170 BRUCE GRIMES
Floor vase 1972, stoneware, 30 in.

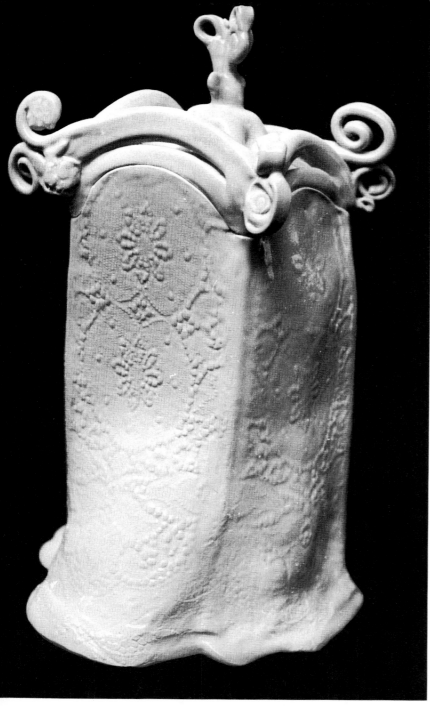

169

170

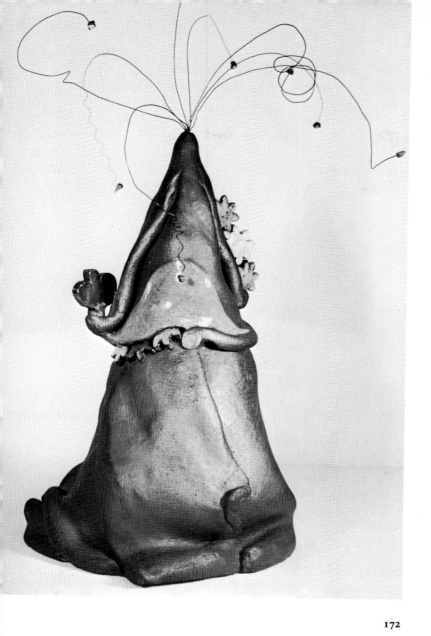

173

171 CLAYTON BAILEY
  '*Demented Pinhead Figurines*' 1971

172 JUDY ONOFRIO
  Construction with wire 1972, stoneware 28 in.

173 DANIEL ENGELKE
  Untitled 1972, stoneware, 4 ft. 10 in.

174 DAVID SHANER
   Teapot 1972, saltglaze

175 HERBERT SANDERS
   Lidded jar 1972, porcelain with crystalline glaze

174

175

172

xi ROBERT M. WINOKUR (U.S.A.)
'*Lidded Jar*' 1972, thrown and hand built porcelain with wood ash glaze, 14 in.

174

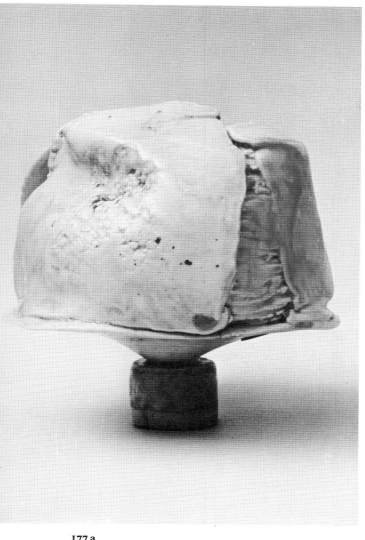

177 a

178

176 ROBERT ARNESON
  'Kiln-man' 1971, terracotta, 36 in.

177 a & b RUTH DUCKWORTH
  Pots 1972, porcelain, 6 in. Photograph
  by Geremy Butler

178 PATTI BAUER
  'Ketchup Kiss' 1972, earthenware clay with low
  fired glaze and lustre decoration, 36 in.

xii PAUL SOLDNER (U.S.A.)
Bottle form 1972, smoked raku, unglazed with
stencilled oxide decoration of potters working,
18 in.

179 DONALD REITZ
Pot 1972, saltglaze, decorated with applied clay, incised
lines, slip and raw oxide, 36 in.

180

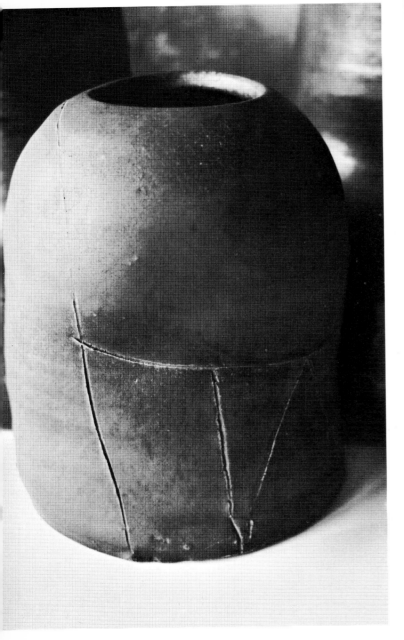

181

180 ROBERT TURNER
Pots 1972, stoneware with sandblasted rust glaze,
10 in. Photograph by Linn Underhill

181 A. C. GARZIO
Casserole 1972, reduced stoneware with volcanic ash
matt glaze, $6\frac{1}{2}$ in.

182 ROBERT RANSOM
'B-Game' 1972, earthenware, 6 in.

183 PAUL SOLDNER
Vase 1971, raku, unglazed, figure drawn decoration
with iron and copper oxide stain over white slip,
smoked after firing, 18 in.

184 JAMES WOZNIAK
'Altered Form' 1972, stoneware, 15 in.

182

183

184

179

South America

Pottery has a long and admirable tradition among the Indians of South America. Especially along the west coast distinctive styles developed using only hand-building methods, until the overthrow of the South American civilizations by Europeans destroyed much traditional work. But potters today are finding inspiration in this early work. The work of the Peruvian Felix Oliva (186) is not a mere copy but builds clearly on tradition. Other potters, at first overwhelmed by the sophisticated working processes and intellectual conceptions of much western pottery, are turning with relief to the more basic work of their own country and are finding in it a fruitful source for their own work.

In Argentina potters use a range of techniques which extends from freely modelled earthenwares, such as the work of Carlos Carle, to slip cast and folded reliefs; Diego Montenegro, one of Argentina's younger potters, uses this technique. Sculptural ceramic objects, some more figurative, others more abstract, also form a considerable part of the work made.

Hilda Goltz, who works in Rio de Janeiro, Brazil, finds inspiration in traditional Aztec work. She models and carves necklaces using Aztec motifs and glazes them with turquoise and purple.

In Venezuela a sophisticated group makes objects which show a keen awareness of events and movements in other countries. Tecla Tofano, in Caracas, makes handbags such as *El Bolso* (188) in earthenware which look almost real. Some potters choose to work in stoneware, while Reina Herera makes spheres and decorates them in a figurative manner which suggests an interest in the work of easel painters.

Throughout South America most large cities have ceramic departments in the art schools. For example in Columbia an active department of ceramics exists at the art school in Bogota.

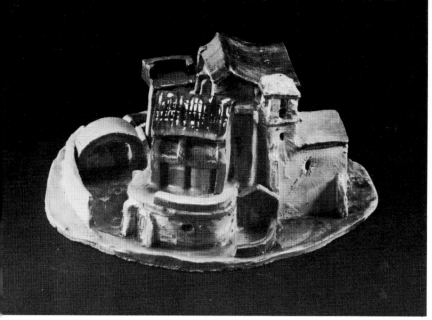

185

186

185 JOHN DAVIS (Peru)
Architectural model 1972, slab-built

186 FELIX OLIVA (Peru)
Pot 1972, stoneware with blue glaze

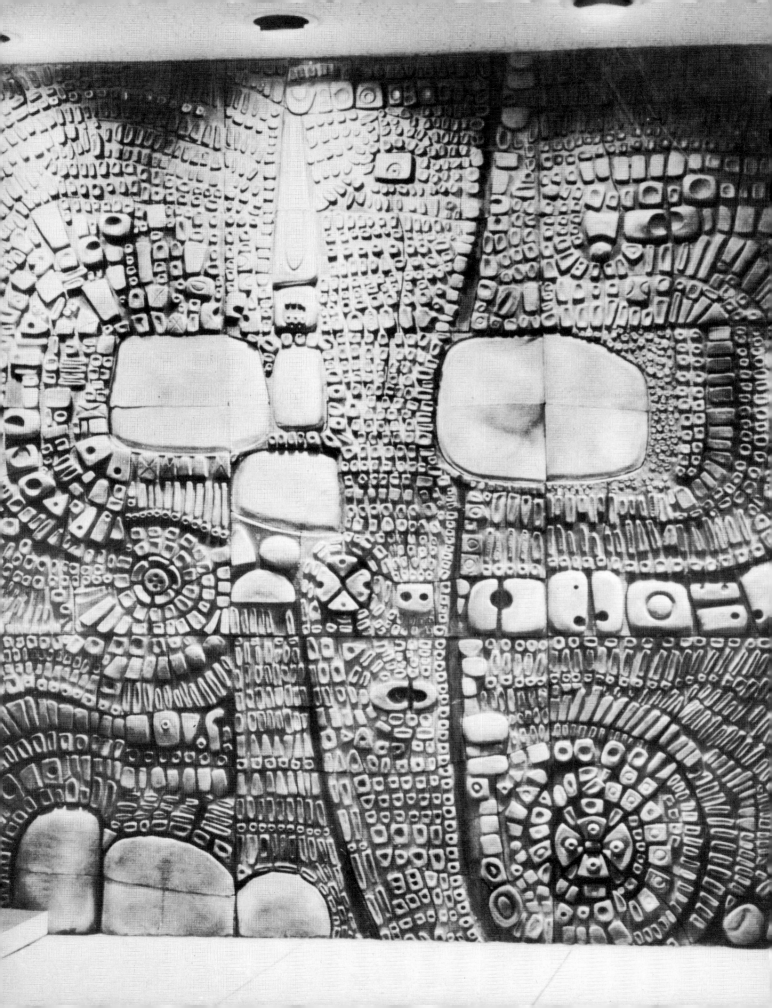

187 EDUARDO VEGA (Ecuador)
'*El callejon Interandino*' 1971, part of mural for City Bank, Quito

188 TECLA TOFANO (Venezuela)
'*El Bolso*' 1972, earthenware body with pale blue and brown
glaze, 9 in. Photograph by Geremy Butler

188

Japan

The history of Japanese ceramics stretches back some 8,000 years. Like most facets of Japanese culture, Japanese ceramics has developed as the result of influence from China and Korea.

Pottery seems to have begun in Japan in what is called the Jōmon ('rope-pattern') period (6000–300 BC). The Jōmon artefacts are richly endowed with the extraordinary creative urges of the early men who learned to harden earth in fire, and the objects seem to be primitive expressions of religious concern. In fact, ceramics did not serve practical daily functions until the Yayoi period (200 BC–AD 300). When the so-called Sue ware was brought in from Korea reduction-fire methods were added to the techniques available and became part of a technical current that still flows today.

The succeeding Kofun period (AD 300–AD 500) concerned itself primarily with the firing of *Haniwa*, or grave ornaments, produced by the earlier oxidation-fire method. When tenmoku and celadon porcelains were introduced from Sung dynasty China, Japanese potters attempted to fashion their own porcelains but failed. In spite of this they succeeded in producing new and indigenous forms of yellow and black Seto pottery. These were used for shrine and temple ornaments and wares, as well as for public tea ceremonies.

In the Azuchi and Momoyama periods of the sixteenth century, Japanese ceramics made many great strides forward. In these turbulent times, violent shifts in governmental power and also in cultural values changed the arts of Japan. The highly aesthetic tea ceremony, as it is known today, grew out of these new values, and a new genre of tea-ware came into being, the Shino, Oribe and other forms, of which Japan is so proud. The influence of the tea ceremony has spread throughout Japanese ceramics, particularly affecting the Bizen and Shigaraki forms. This influence continues even to this day.

In the interregnum between the Momoyama and Edo periods, which took up the last years of the sixteenth century, Japanese ceramists imported the two-colour, contrasted ware of the Chosen style from Korea and fired their own imitations of it locally. The Karatsu, Hagi and Satsuma wares are very similar even today.

During the Edo period, which extended from AD 1600 to the opening of Japan to the West, the Japanese learned how to make the Korean cobalt-blue porcelains and the Chinese enamel overglazed wares: porcelain gradually replaced many of the lower fired wares. The white body and five-colour overglazes which Japanese potters were formerly incapable of creating was combined with the flamboyant spirit of the Edo culture to create an even more extravagant style.

With the Meiji period, beginning in 1868, Japan came under the western influence. In accordance with the slogans of the time, 'National prosperity and military strength', and 'Production through industry', the Meiji government swiftly established trade with the West and made ceramics one of its principal

xiii KAZUO YAGI (Japan)
'*Night Offering*' 1970, width 16 in. Photograph
by Naomi Maki

exports. 'China' became a product of Japan, rather than of the country from which it derived its name.

The inculcation of Western technical expertise was rapid, but not until about the middle of the twentieth century did Western ideas about artistic individuality and originality take hold among Japanese potters. As a result Japanese ceramics have only recently developed along lines similar to the rest of the modern world, clearing the way for potters like Kawai, Kitaoji, Hamada, and Tomimoto.

These men shared a belief in the individual consciousness, although at the same time they strove to maintain and even reproduce the work of earlier masters. Turning to the past, they attempted to produce an art that would be timeless. The fact that they escaped the triviality into which Japanese ceramics usually falls when it becomes concerned with traditionalism is a testament to their greatness.

Today Japan is an unparalleled haven for potters. At present, at least 400 potters can support themselves as ceramic artists. Barely a week goes by in Tokyo in which there are not at least four or five ceramic shows running concurrently. Recently a show by one famous potter sold almost its entire stock of tea bowls, averaging $10,000 a bowl, on the first day. It is not only that the Japanese love pottery, they are also prepared to invest in it and to acquire it as a status symbol. Of course, a certain number love ceramics blindly, and there are potters who make every effort to avoid disillusioning them: their activities are but symptomatic of a period of ceramic popularity hitherto unknown.

And yet what does Japan have to be proud about in the seventies? Its art has behind it the greatness of Jōmon, Yayoi, Haniwa, Shino, Kutani and the rest, but when we attempt to find in contemporary work a link with these illustrious predecessors, we find a curious loneliness at the centre of this flourishing ceramic activity. Japan may have some of the finest pottery in the world, but it is almost entirely dependent on reproducing past forms or devising clever modern gimmickry. Looking at modern Japanese culture we fail to find pottery that is sensitive to the needs of that culture and able to lead it towards a satisfaction of those needs.

Surely, no people, who have created a proud tradition in a particular art, have maintained that tradition without constantly returning to the original source for inspiration and instruction. Yet contemporary Japanese ceramics has not surpassed the achievements of earlier times, and seems content to meet the problems of today in rather a feeble manner. Now, culture should respond to the demands of its time. If it lets the opportunity pass by, the rhythm of life is weakened, and the arts become simply a battle between differing techniques, the pursuit of form, and finally emptiness. Most modern Japanese ceramics are moving in this direction, a direction in which only artistic introspection and aesthetic triviality are to be found.

In many ways cultural traditions are sacred. Yet culture must be constantly involved in the process of creation. If cultural tradition is continued unthinkingly, it has no possibility of development.

With the end of World War II Japan entered a period in which she lost much of her cultural confidence. Values underwent great fluctuations and through many variations. The war had barely ended when a movement calling itself the Sōdeisha, centering around Kazuo Yagi, Osamu Suzuki and Junkichi Kumakura, sprang up in Kyoto. They cut their ties with the rigidly formalized tea aesthetics, turned away from function and purpose in art, and entered the ceramic world ready to criticize and to oppose – in fact to espouse the very opposite of what the conservative ceramic establishment believed at that time.

These ceramics were soon attacked from various directions, and the new movement received little attention. These new ceramists seemed to be simply a small group of outsiders, standing quite apart from the flourishing main stream of ceramic activity. However their ideas were part of the great intellectual ferment of the time, and are mentioned here because they form part of my own inquiry.

Secondly, a folk craft movement, in which the implements of everyday life were seen as things of value, initiated a movement calling for the creation of these implements. This soon gave way to the 'appreciation' movement, in which function found itself secondary in importance to the allure of clay and the beauty of handwork. In the background a new set of values had come with the cultural changes of the time that placed great store by the usefulness and the materials of hand-made goods. This set of values was closely related to the fact that crafts had lost their viability in the face of competition from machine-made goods. From a practical point of view they had, in fact, become useless, obsolete.

Once, woodblocks had been the basic implements of printing, but when they were replaced by metal-type set by machines, the woodblock became a medium in its own right and paved the way for the highly expressive woodblock print. Calligraphy, that had once been a basic method of communication using ideographs and pictographs, gave way to printing and type, and the path towards the appreciation of calligraphy opened. Similarly, a new approach to ceramics was brought about by the growing move away from the production of hand-made household articles and implements and by the new value placed upon workmanship and materials. One can see how this change came about once mass-production methods could satisfy economic demands; and also how ceramics, in which the skills of workmanship and the beauty of the materials had become more important than the function of the object, came to acquire qualitative rather than quantitative values, and aesthetic rather than practical values. This was, in a way, the path towards a new art, one in which function had neither positive nor negative significance.

Today, what is something that requires only clay and the hand for its manufacture? Should it be attributed with new values? What meaning is there in adapting clay to various restricting conditions? By answering these questions in the context of modern civilization we can grope our way to a new art form.

'Nature has been rooted out; pollution has shortened life. In the face of this can human life be extended?' While human beings utter these words, the threat

xiv MUTSUO YANAGIHARA (Japan)
'*Flower Vase*' 1971

to human life goes on. Yet the Japanese people continue working as loyally as ever for their corporation, their country, or to win the economic war. From this they can only derive hollow pride in an empty achievement.

The potter who has no other path to tread save that of art must understand civilization and history, and from this understanding define his attitude so that he can follow his own path. In this way, he can respond to man's present aspirations with understanding and echo its vibrations. This is surely the essence of modern ceramics.

Some potters at work in Japan, who are illustrated here, have developed, in accordance with the conditions of modern civilization, a new language. They know the folly of ignoring tradition. They also know the dangers of falling into a facile modernism. Since they are trying to fulfil their responsibilities as living, breathing human beings in the modern world, in them lie, I believe, the new potentialities of Japanese ceramics. The new direction they have chosen is a lonely one in modern Japanese life.

Kimpei Nakamura

Tokyo 1973

189

189 RYUSAKU MIWA
    '*Man of eye*' 1972, 12 in.

190 KIMPEI NAKAMURA
    '*Teapot*' 1972, rust and gold with white handle,
    10 in. Photograph by K. Nakamura

191 KAZUO YAGI
    '*Ocean*' 1970, black pottery, 19 in.

192 OSAMU SUZUKI
    '*Square Bird*' 1971, rust glaze, 12 in.

190

190

191

192

193

194

193 SEIMEI TSUJI
'*Crab*' 1972, stoneware incense case with
natural ash glaze, 1½ in.

194 KIMPEI NAKAMURA
'*Mural*' 1972, white glaze, 3 yd × 15 yd
Photograph by T. Shimoda

195 KAZUO YAGI
'*Painted Pot*' 1971, inlay decoration and iron
marking, 12 in.

196 RYOJI KOIE
'*Return to the Earth*' 1971

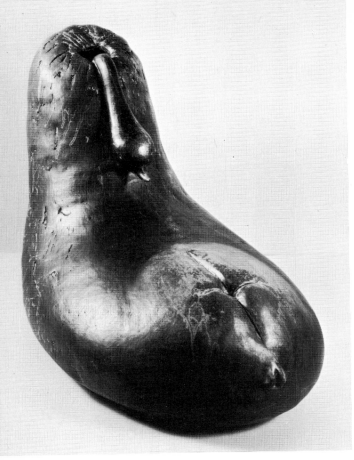

197 JUNKICHI KUMAKURA
   'Bird B' 1972, brownish yellow glaze, 21 in.

198 JUNKICHI KUMAKURA
   'Portrait' 1971, brownish yellow glaze, 19 in.

199 SEIMEI THUJI
   'Pottery Box' 1970, stoneware with natural
   ash glaze, 10 in.

200 MUTSUO YANAGIHARA
   Flower vase 1971, gold and blue decoration

198

194

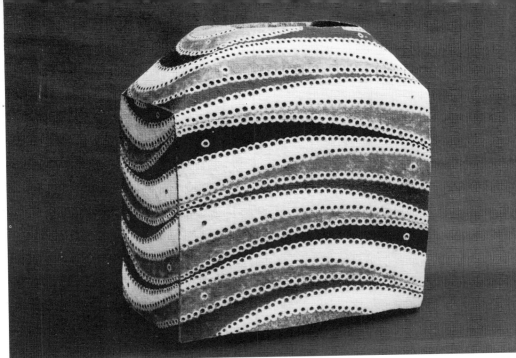

201

202

201 SHOJI KAMOTA
Pot 1972, with green, white and blue
decoration

202 SHOJI KAMOTA
Object 1970, dark grey body, no glaze,
13 in.

xv OSAMU SUZUKI (Japan)
'*Horse*' 1972, stoneware, 30 in.

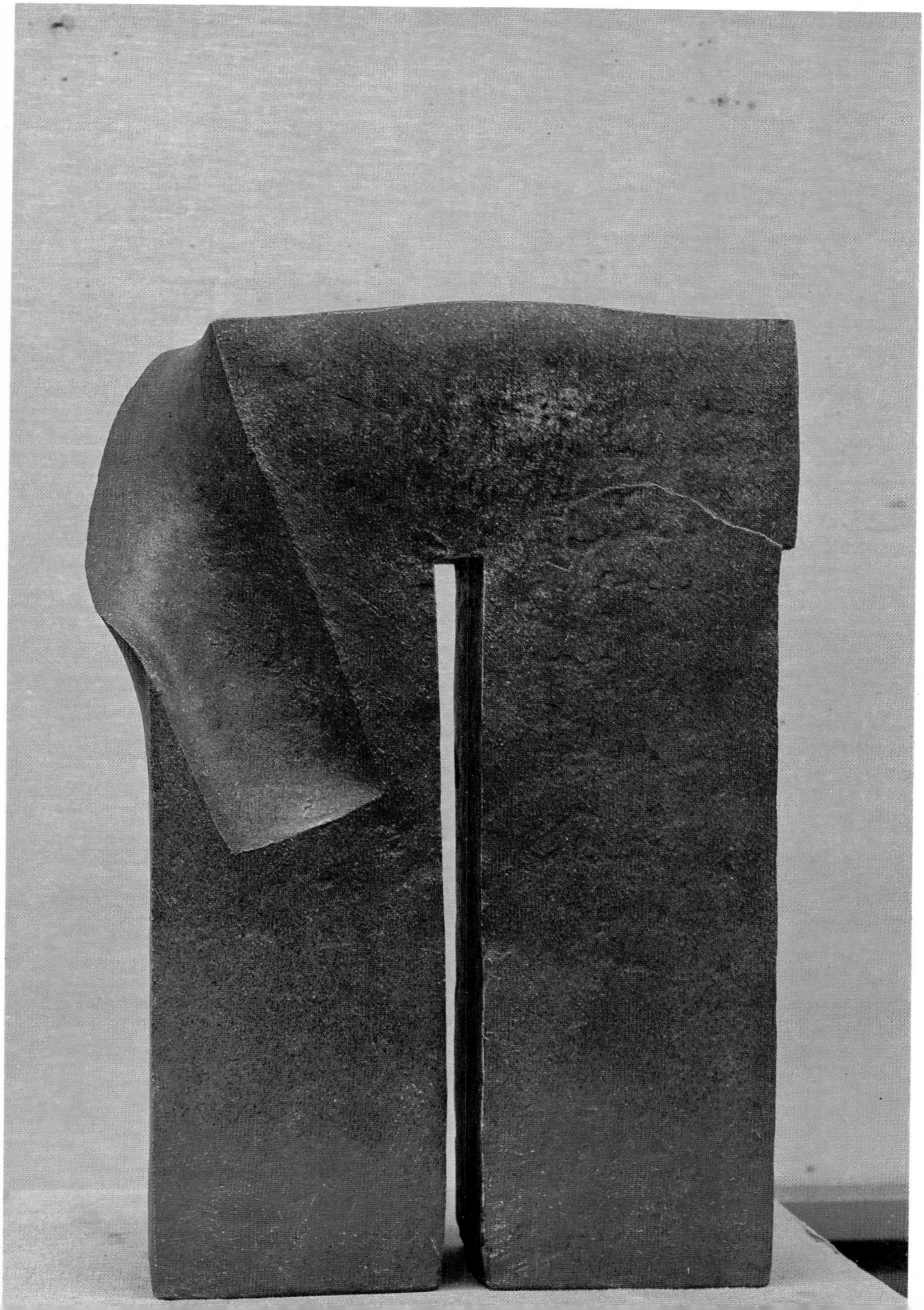

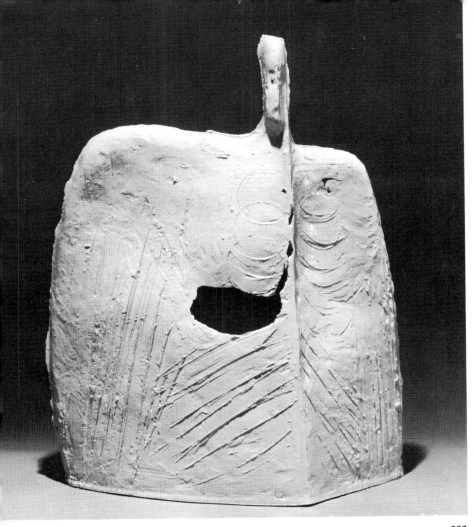

203

204

205

206

203 GORO KAWAMOTO
Object 1970, white porcelain 24 in.

204 HIDETO SATONAKA
'Pollution Allergy' 1971, 12 in.

205 RYOKI KOIE
'Return to the Earth' 1972

206 SHOJI HAMADA
Square dish 1972, reduced stoneware with trailed
copper green glaze over khaki brown, width
12½ in. Collection of Victoria and Albert Museum,
London; photograph by Geremy Butler

207 GORO KAWAMOTO
Pot 1970, stoneware with dark aquamarine ash glaze,
12 in.

207

199

xvi PETER TRAVIS (Australia)
Dish 1972, earthenware clay with oxides and a
matt glaze, width 23 in. Photograph by
Douglas Thompson

Australia
and New Zealand

Although Australia and New Zealand are close geographically, and although their potters were at first similarly influenced by the English and Japanese ceramic traditions which flowed to them through the writings and philosophy of Bernard Leach, yet the work of the major craftsmen in both countries manifest distinct differences of approach. Many of these stem from the personal vision of the potters themselves, some of whom have taken as their criteria the art of primitive man, others the pottery of Japanese Jōmon or Chinese Shang. While the symbolism of New Guinea masks and Maori totem figures have inspired certain clay creations, others have drawn ceramic comment out of the complexities and confusions of the atomic age. In the absence of a historical tradition of their own potters have borrowed, whether consciously or unconsciously, from art and craft of others. Yet they have placed the stamp of individuality on their work, making it recognizable as a personal statement rather than part of a national movement.

While the potters of both countries produce work of individual interest, as well as work of a utilitarian nature, it is interesting to note a changing emphasis in response to altered conditions. Whereas at one time the New Zealanders commanded a wider public acceptance for their own domestic pottery than did the Australians, the great increase in the number of trained potters in Australia has narrowed this gap so much that they cannot even keep up with the present demand for useful pots, more often producing better designed ware for the home than the factory product.

In the formative years in New Zealand, when the government placed severe restrictions on imported ceramics, there was a strong public demand for individual domestic ware. This enabled the potter to work full-time to supply that demand, while his Australian counterpart could not survive as a potter only and had to turn to teaching to support himself. The production of domestic pottery in New Zealand not only gave the potters a living but helped the public to appreciate good functional ware made by their own craftsmen. The situation of the Australians, who had accepted the fact of full-time teaching and who in their own work had to compete with a great quantity of industrial domestic products, forced them to take a different view. They turned to highly individual and imaginative concepts for their expressions in clay and their influence on the public was largely in this direction.

Because of this sustained emphasis on the teaching areas in pottery, from primary school to technical college, Australia now has a very great number of potters, most of whom have had a fair to excellent training. From the thousands of students only a dedicated few persist long enough to reach professional level, the few who are prepared to discipline themselves with hard work until they discover through long experience what they want to say in clay. The rest enjoy making pots with no inclination to make it a life-time's work; others go no further than learning to appreciate pottery. During the last ten to fifteen years there has been a growth in these divisions of interest together with an increasingly informed attitude from the buying public. Good quality domestic ware with an individual accent has had a ready market, and at the same time the artist potter has been able to pursue his excursions in experiment and imagery to the full; both types of work are accepted, and indeed demanded, in contemporary Australia.

Over the last two decades the standard and type of tuition given by Australian technical colleges reflects in the calibre of the final year student. All colleges are undergoing change at present with the range of requirements expanding rapidly, and from the changing curricula we are already seeing new attitudes and new concepts in ceramics, tentative though they are.

Foremost among the colleges is the National Art School in Sydney, New South Wales, whose department of ceramics is served by some of the major teaching potters in Australia. Peter Rushforth (218) has headed this school for twenty odd years, the flexibility of his approach allowing a diversity of talent to flourish and grow. Prominent potters such as Col Levy, Bernard Sahm, Shiga Shigeo, Peter Travis, Derek Smith (212) and Gillian Grigg are members of the staff. Mollie Douglas, Joan Grounds and Stephen Skillitzi (211) among others have taught there, and Ivan Englund (216), now head teacher of painting in the school, previously headed the ceramics department at the Wollongong Technical College. The National Art School has largely influenced and set the pace for schools in other states, and the strong core of potters in Sydney has, through the running of summer schools, shared techniques and ideas with potters all over the continent who have travelled thousands of miles to take these intensive pottery courses and returned home to teach others in similar schools of their own. From the Sydney base, potteries have been organized throughout New South Wales in Technical Schools and Colleges of Advanced Education. As well as giving training in ceramics these schools especially cater for creative leisure classes. This is a new approach in the technical education sphere since the authorities are prepared to take the lead with encouragement and enthusiasm.

Experiment in ceramics is part of the curriculum in most colleges, and students are influenced by current art movements to express in clay and related media their conception of 'international art', though this is largely imitative as yet and somewhat in a minor key. The South Australian College of Art has produced some interesting work from its ceramic department under Milton Moon (219), as have the graduates from the Sydney colleges. In Perth Joan Campbell (217), with her enthusiasm for large raku pieces, has had considerable influence. Many of the more advanced experimenters have only just set up studios and it can be expected that future work in ceramics will be different again from that which is illustrated here.

Potters' groups are to be found in all states, as small country groupings and large city societies flourish in the present enthusiasm for the hand-made pot. Leading potters belong to the Potters' Society of Australia, which was founded in 1956 by Ivan McMeekin, Mollie Douglas, Ivan Englund and Peter Rushforth, and has expanded into a society of exhibiting, associate and student members. Run on a non-profit basis it has undertaken all the obligations that such a group demands, viz. a teaching workshop and an exhibition gallery with a continous showing of members' work; a biennial selective exhibition for all members; the publication of the magazine, *Pottery in Australia*, which serves some 5,000 potters throughout Australia and overseas, and booklets on technical requirements for kilns, wheels and so on; the sponsoring and arrangement of tours and exhibitions in Australia by internationally known potters such as Michael Cardew, Harry Davis and Paul Soldner, Shoji Hamada, Tatsuzo Shimaoka and Takeichi Kawai – Bernard Leach being the first of the visitors in 1962, when the New Zealand and Australian potters combined to arrange his tour.

Other ceramic groups in Sydney, Melbourne, Brisbane, Adelaide and Perth bring together potters to discuss and give practical demonstrations of work in a spirit of camaraderie. Groups in all states are on the move. Within them the specialist potters tend to concentrate on their own work, but are prepared to give advice and help when called upon. Such a potter is Ivan McMeekin who, by his experimental work in Australian clay and glaze materials, has benefited not only the Industrial Arts Department of the University of New South Wales, where he teaches, but potters everywhere.★ H. R. and R. R. Hughan (father and son) and Ian Sprague (210) in Victoria have used their knowledge to encourage new potters, as have Eileen Keys in Western Australia, David Smith, Mervyn Feeney and Harry Memmott in Queensland, and many potters in other states.

Most of the outstanding Australian potters are also teachers, sought after for seminars and schools all over the continent; many undertake architectural commissions and special projects, some have influential liaison with industry, and all present major exhibitions of their work regularly. Their aspirations and their problems are similar to those of the New Zealand potters but the influences determining the course of pottery in New Zealand differ in some respects.

New Zealand pottery emerged in the fifties, in most instances as a hobby enterprise. Thanks to the New Zealand Association of Art Societies travel grants to outstanding potters, such as Len Castle (227) and Peter Stichbury (226), who went overseas for further study with Bernard Leach and Michael Cardew, the early influences were undoubtedly of the Leach-Hamada type, as they were also in Australia at that time.

The divergence in the two countries has partly centred upon the teaching problem, which Australia enjoys and New Zealand does not. Even now, New Zealand has no school of ceramics and no school of art includes pottery as a course, while few secondary schools encourage children to work in clay.

★ See his: *Notes for potters in Australia, vol. I: raw materials and clay bodies*, University of New South Wales Press, Sydney 1967.

However, at all the Teachers' Colleges there are excellent teachers of pottery who give some training in ceramics to students majoring in other subjects, and many of the present full-time potters have been students at these Colleges.

With no full teaching courses available, potters in New Zealand have necessarily had to share their knowledge, and they have been grateful for the guidance and help of the visiting celebrities, Hamada, Leach, Kawai and Cardew. Perhaps one of the strongest influences on New Zealand pottery came with the arrival in 1962 of Harry and May Davis from England and the establishment of their Crewenna Pottery at Nelson, as the dedication and competence of this team making a living by fine domestic pots gave an example to all. Two years later, also at Nelson, Jack Laird, another Englishman, set up his semi-industrial workshop where he now employs seventeen people. Most New Zealand potters make functional articles for reasons set out earlier in this introduction. There are very few who do not make containers of one sort or another and only a small handful has launched forth into ceramic sculpture and 'expressionism'. The fact that there are nearly one hundred full-time potters who earn a living by their pots (some perhaps only at subsistence level) in a population of three million is well worth recording. The few who, like David Brokenshire and Neil Grant (225), have gone in for more sculptural pieces are not dependent on their ceramics for a living, and in fact it would be hard to survive in this sphere only. Perhaps it is for this reason that New Zealand potters, with very few exceptions, have left this field severely alone.

Mention must be made of those outstanding potters who have exhibited both in New Zealand and abroad, for they have had a marked influence on their countrymen. Auckland, the most active centre for pottery in New Zealand, boasts such figures as Len Castle, Peter Stichbury, Patricia Perrin, Yvonne Rust and Graeme Storm; Wellington has Doreen Blumhardt, Roy Cowan (224) and Mirek Smisek (223); from Coromandel come Barrie Brickell and Warren Tippet, and Helen Mason from Hawke's Bay. All these outstanding potters teach according to their special spheres of interest. Roy Cowan is best known for his architectural commissions and his research into kilns and raw materials, and Peter Stichbury excels in the production of functional pottery. Len Castle's work indicates his interest in organic forms using fine technical skills and a creative imagination, and Mirek Smisek's combination of salt and stoneware glazes also leads in this direction. Teaching either privately or at evening classes, Teachers' Colleges of summer schools, their influence on students is evidence of their ability and concern in the absence of full-time courses.

An educational focal point both for potters and public has been the Annual New Zealand Exhibition. From 1957 when Oswald Stephens and the Visual Arts Association organized the first New Zealand Studio Potters' Exhibition in Dunedin with fifteen invited potters, this annual showing of work from all over New Zealand, alternating between four main cities, has had a very wide influence. As a direct result of such exhibitions by voluntary groups, the New Zealand Society of Potters was formed in order to plan future activities and to serve the potters' interests. For similar reasons the magazine, *The New Zealand*

Potter, was founded by Helen Mason and was edited by her for ten years. Now edited by Margaret Harris, it has kept New Zealanders informed about potters and their work.

Obviously, self-help, trial and error, and the sharing of knowledge have been the main contributing factors in the present status of pottery in New Zealand, plus the influence of Leach, Cardew, and Davis with their emphasis on the craftsman's approach. In contrast, Australians have come by their knowledge through the disciplines of their teaching institutions, which have adopted new modes of approach to give great latitude to creative potters. In both instances the teachers themselves have been the foremost potters of their day.

The whole new movement of the artist craftsman in pottery has gathered impulse over the last ten years in both countries, and it is those who have had the advantage of time in accumulating knowledge and experience, expressing with technical ease and imaginative mind the force of their creative ability, who are represented in this book.

Wanda Garnsey

New South Wales 1973

Australia

208 MAREA GAZZARD (Australia)
   Objects and pots 1972, white stoneware body, about
   26 in. Photograph by Donald Gazzard

209 VICTOR GREENAWAY (Australia)
   Spiral form with sphere 1971, stoneware body with
   brown and grey glaze, 21 in. Photograph by
   Geremy Butler

210 IAN SPRAGUE (Australia)
   Pot 1972, stoneware with applied and incised decoration, ash glaze, 10 in. Photograph by Mark Strizic

211 STEPHEN SKILLITZI (Australia)
Organic form 1972, earthenware body
with reduced copper red glaze, 12 in.
Photograph by Douglas Thompson

212 DEREK SMITH (Australia)
Vase 1969, stoneware body with grey
and blue glaze, $11\frac{1}{2}$ in. Photograph by
Geremy Butler

213 SUZANNE FORSYTH (Australia)
Objects 1972, stoneware with oxide
decoration, 14–20 in. Photograph by
Douglas Thompson

215

214 JUDY LORRAINE (Australia)
Object 1972, stoneware, no glaze, with iron
pigment, 8 in. Photograph by Douglas Thompson

215 LES BLAKEBROUGH (Australia)
Lidded pot 1972, stoneware body with
Mittagong rock glaze fired in wood kiln, 12 in.
Photograph by Douglas Thompson

216 IVAN ENGLUND (Australia)
Bottle 1972, stoneware body with added rock
fragments, 12 in. Photograph by Douglas
Thompson

216

217 JOAN CAMPBELL (Australia)
Pot 1971, raku body with soft grey slip, smoked in gum leaves after firing, 18 in. Photograph by Douglas Thompson

218 PETER RUSHFORTH (Australia)
Blossom jar 1971, saltglaze stoneware with green and brown surface, 9 in. Photograph by Geremy Butler

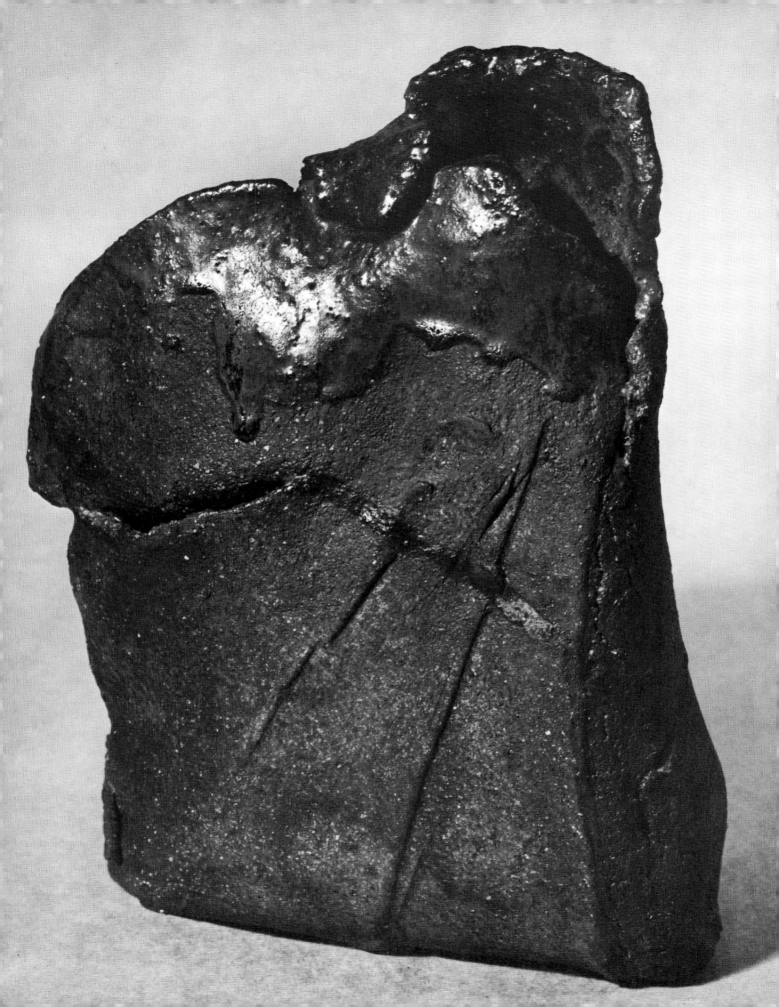

219 MILTON MOON (Australia)
Form 1972, reduced stoneware, using Queensland Bundamba clay with ash glaze, 10 in. Photograph by Douglas Thompson

220 ALAN PEASCOD (Australia)
Covered jar 1971, stoneware body with buff and brown matt glaze, 13 in. Photograph by Geremy Butler

220

221

221 WANDA GARNSEY (Australia)
Punch bowl 1972, reduced stoneware
with blue/black slip under ash type
glaze, 18 in. Photograph by Douglas
Thompson

222 GILLIAN GRIGG (Australia)
Dish 1972, reduced stoneware with
spotted gum tree ash glaze, 18 in.
Photograph by Douglas Thompson

222

New Zealand

223 MIREK SMISEK (New Zealand)
Lidded jar 1972, saltglaze stoneware with iron
slip, 20 in. Photograph by Stan Jenkins

224 ROY COWAN (New Zealand)
Mural, for Europa House, Wellington; stone-
ware and porcelain tiles, 12 ft × 15 ft.
Photograph by Ans Westra

223

224

225 NEIL GRANT (New Zealand)
Pot 1972, reduced stoneware with band of dry
glaze decoration, width 27 in.

226 PETER STICHBURY (New Zealand)
Bottle 1972, reduced stoneware with brushed black
oxide decoration, 23 in. Photograph by Ans Westra

227 LEN CASTLE (New Zealand)
Hanging bottles 1970, reduced unglazed stoneware
body with brown and grey colouring, 9 in.

227

Bibliography

Beard, Geoffrey *Modern Ceramics*. Studio Vista, London 1969 and Dutton, New York

Birks, Tony *The Art of the Modern Potter*. Country Life Books, Feltham, Middlesex 1970

Charleston, Robert J. (ed.) *World Ceramics: Illustrated History*. Hamlyn, Feltham, Middlesex 1968

Cooper, Emmanuel *History of Pottery*. Longman, Harlow, Essex 1972 and St Martin's Press, New York

Hettěs, K. and Rada, P. *Modern Ceramics*. London 1965

Leach, Bernard *A Potter's Book*. Faber & Faber, London 1945 and Transatlantic Arts, New York

Rose, Muriel *Artist Potters in England*. Faber & Faber, London 1970

Magazines
Ceramic Review, 5 Belsize Lane, London NW3 5AD, UK
Ceramics Monthly, Box 4548, Columbus, Ohio 43212, USA
Craft Horizons, 44 West 53rd Street, New York, New York 10019, USA
Crafts, 12 Waterloo Place, London SW1Y 4SU, UK
New Zealand Potter, Box 12–162, Wellington North, New Zealand
Pottery in Australia, 30 Turramurra Avenue, New South Wales 2074, Australia
Pottery Quarterly, Northfield Studio, Tring, Hertfordshire, UK
Studio Potter, Box 172, Warner, N. H. 03278, USA
Tactile, The Canadian Guild of Potters Inc., 100 Avenue Road, Toronto, Ontario, Canada

Index

Numbers in italics refer to illustrations